PIRATE WISDOM

PIRATE WISDOM

✦

Lessons in navigating the high seas of your organization

Elisa S. Robyn, Ph.D.
Cindy L. Miles, Ph.D.

iUniverse, Inc.
New York Lincoln Shanghai

PIRATE WISDOM
Lessons in navigating the high seas of your organization

Copyright © 2006 by Elisa Robyn & Cindy Miles

All rights reserved. No part of this book may be used or reproduced by any means, graphic, electronic, or mechanical, including photocopying, recording, taping or by any information storage retrieval system without the written permission of the publisher except in the case of brief quotations embodied in critical articles and reviews.

iUniverse books may be ordered through booksellers or by contacting:

iUniverse
2021 Pine Lake Road, Suite 100
Lincoln, NE 68512
www.iuniverse.com
1-800-Authors (1-800-288-4677)

ISBN-13: 978-0-595-40558-9 (pbk)
ISBN-13: 978-0-595-84923-9 (ebk)
ISBN-10: 0-595-40558-4 (pbk)
ISBN-10: 0-595-84923-7 (ebk)

Printed in the United States of America

Contents

I. Why Pirate Wisdom?..1

II. Set Yer Course..5

III. The Pirate Wisdom Code..................................7
    The Lesson of Political Savvy...........................7
    The Lesson of Destiny...................................9
    The Lesson of Energy....................................9
    The Lesson of Workplace Politics.......................10
    The Lesson of Rules....................................11
    The Lesson of Freedom..................................13

IV. Pirate Basics..14
    How to Tell if Yer a Pirate............................14
    Know Yer Ship and Ocean................................15
    Know the Players.......................................15
    Know the Crew..16
    Know Yerself...17
    Choose Yer Role..18
    Keep a Captain's Log...................................19
    Reading the Map..20
    Hunting for Treasure...................................20
    Enjoy Yer Treasure.....................................21
    Hoist the Jolly Roger..................................22
    Aim for Madness or Brilliance..........................23
    Make Yer Weakness Yer Strength.........................25
    Set Yer Own Rules......................................25

Hold Yer Line 27

V. Leading the Crew 29
Keep Yer Crew Hardy 29
Managing By Pirating Around 30
Create a Community of Power 30
Be the Common Vision 32
Be the Leader Yer Crew Believes In 32
Developing the Crew 33
Share the Booty 35
Never Fight on the Ship 36
Crime and Punishment 37
Down a Cup of Grog 38

VI. Sailing the Ship 40
Count Yer Doubloons 40
Sail in the Direction of the Strategic Plan 41
Pirate the Dominant Language 41
Take Responsibility 43
Tacking Upwind 43
Attend to Lighthouses and Foghorns 44
Never Sail Over a Shallow Reef 44
Sail Close to the Wind (Very Advanced Pirating) 45
Get to Dry Dock 46

VII. Navigating the Waters 47
Know Which Rules to Break and Which to Bend 47
Build Relationships in Every Port 48
Give Room at the Mark 48
Know How Yer Enemies Sail 49
Practice the Art of Misdirection 50
Play to Their Chinks, Protect Yer Chinks 51
Remember Everyone Likes to Dress Up 52
Beware of Mermaids and Sirens 53
Pirates and the Butterfly Effect 54

    Use Yer Letters of Marques 55
    When and How to Mutiny 55
    No Raping or Pillaging 56
    Take Yer Due 57
    Take Piratically Wild Risks 58

VIII. Pirates and Queens 60

IX. Maintaining Safe Port 62
    Garnering Safe Port From the Queen 62
    Garnering Safe Port From Others 63
    Garnering Safe Port With Fellow Pirates 65
    Keep Yer Own Private Island 65

X. "X" Marks the Spot 67
    Remember Why You Want to be a Pirate 67
    Getting Yer Treasure 68

Resources 71

*See the world as it is.
Live in the world as it should be.
Invite others into the sea of possibility.*

Chapter 1

Why Pirate Wisdom?

This is a handbook about how to become a better leader or member of your organization by becoming a good pirate. By *good*, we mean both effective and decent. Good pirates know how to steer their professional and personal lives. They are first-class stewards of their ships, clear about where they are going, and facile navigators of changing winds and waters. Good pirates also ascribe to the Greek philosophy that happiness is our highest moral duty. Good pirates pursue the good life. They seek sound ships, trustworthy comrades, engaging adventures, safe harbors, and treasure enough for the day. At times they may be wild and wily, but they respect a code of honor, and they know that the true treasure they seek is life itself. They answer the perennial bidding of the soul by following Joseph Campbell's advice to "follow your bliss." And they sense, as Campbell taught, that what we yearn for is not the meaning of life, but a feeling of aliveness. Good pirates seek to feel alive and to express that aliveness in all they do.

Our brand of pirate is more Robin Hood than Blackbeard, more Jimmy Buffet than Donald Trump, more Gandhi than Machiavelli. The pirate wisdom we share is the art and craft of navigating the world of work, whether from the perspective of leader or member of the crew. It will not help you pilfer, pillage, plunder, or hijack the corner office. Pirate wisdom helps you recognize and navigate the political waters in which you sail every day, and do so artfully, playfully, and purposefully. It guides you to set a clear course of action and to develop skills in adaptability and resilience in the face of the dynamic complexity (some call it instability) and rapid change (some say chaos) that marks today's organizations. It shows you how to take wild but calculated risks and gives you strategies for becoming a good pirate as a crew member, captain, king, or queen.

Above all, pirate wisdom helps you become savvier at managing people and relationships—the perennially political dimensions of any organization—the stuff at which pirates particularly excel. So what does it mean to be politically savvy? It means that you are adroit at following the threads in a complex political web. You swiftly assess any situation you walk into. You see the games and dynamics at play, and you are immune to their attraction. You know how to play, but you create your own rules. You recognize that your choices and actions create your world and that you have a role in your destiny. You take important risks and have a bit of fun shaking up the status quo for appropriate ends. You ride the waves of change and sometimes create them. You go through each day conscious of your power to shape the lives of the people you touch and the organization in which you work. Ultimately, as a politically savvy pirate, you know you can operate happily and well in any system, with the understanding that systems, rules, players, and circumstances always change.

This book is based on our observation that every work environment—whether a multinational corporation, a nonprofit organization, an educational enterprise, a church, an office, a shop, or a family business—is a political ecosystem. And pirates, at least the kind we study and promote, are masters of surviving and thriving in political environs. These pirates seek a good life, but recognize the inexorable interdependence of all systems. Even if they don't use such terms, effective pirates have figured out the human and power structures in their organizations and know how to navigate these systems to get where they want to go.

Pirate wisdom honors classic concepts about the connectedness of life and draws from multiple fields of thought that reflect archetypal and contemporary explanations of interrelatedness and how the world works: ecology, systems theory, collective and multiple intelligence, chaos theory, social constructivism, and synchronicity. Just as these approaches to science, art, and spirituality link ancient and modern thought, our pirates bridge old and new organizational paradigms.

We have been developing our pirate skills for a number of years, in alternating roles as captain, queen, and crewmember. But we did not set sail to become pirates all at once. Our foray into the world of pirating started in a college where we worked together as administrators. One semester, when we were facing particularly tough financial cutbacks and new state regulations that demanded major modifications in how we ran the college, Elisa began using a pirate metaphor to help bring her department together to face these changes. She referred to her academic center as a ship dubbed *Paradigm,* which she captained as the Pirate Dean under the Jolly Roger of Arts and Sciences. She talked to her faculty and staff about finding new treasure, holding true to the code, and navigating rough seas. Suddenly, the metaphor filled our sails, and we set off with Jimmy Buffet, Johnny Depp, and Captain Morgan as comic models.

Pirate flags and ships appeared on office doors, sea shanties were hummed in the halls, and pirate banter infused our meetings: "Arrrr! This here meeting will come to order." "All ye sea dogs best get yer reports in by Friday, else ye be scurvy scum." But the playfulness led to serious conversations about leadership and survival in real-life political oceans. We found ourselves talking about what moved us as individuals and as a college, how we could follow our moral code without wavering in turbulent seas, how we could follow the navy's rules but lead from the edges of the armada, how we could inspire a crew to be present and powerful, and how we could always slow down to find the steadfast compass within us. Our deeper conversations would break the surface again as pirate playfulness, and then dive back in for explorations into innovation, synchronicity, learning institutions, and navigating organizational politics and change.

Which would lead us back to the pirate life. We lashed onto pirating as a buoy in rough waters and discovered a course to deep truths.

Since then, each time we share our ideas about pirate wisdom with a new audience, we find a shift in the group's energy from struggle and frustration with organizational challenges we dub the *Land of What Is* to excitement about the *Piratical Art of Possibility*. Almost always, we encounter an enthusiastic affinity with the metaphor, once folks realize we don't promote mutiny, looting, or walking adversaries off the plank. Seemingly everyone wants to play pirate. Witness the millions of people worldwide who join in *Talk Like a Pirate Day* celebrations each September 19th. Arr, me hearties!

In this book, we will walk you through the initial lessons we teach in Pirate School: the theory and rationale of pirating; first steps (Pirating 101), including getting to know yourself, your queen (or king), your crew, your ship, the waters in which you choose to sail; how to develop and manage a crew; sailing your ship; navigating political waters; maintaining safe port; and finding and enjoying your treasure. We open our personal treasure chests of piratical principles, strategies, and tools to help you navigate your own capricious winds of political and organizational change.

We hope this book helps make your personal and professional life more meaningful and enjoyable. At the end of the day, like all good pirates, we're in it for the freedom, the fortune, the glory, and, most of all, the fun. We hope you'll enjoy the voyage. So, welcome aboard, mates. Now, hoist ye the mainsail!

Chapter 2

Set Yer Course

When we talk about pirating we are talking about a way of being present in the world. Being a pirate is a holistic process. It is not a series of individual linear choices about where to sail and how to get the treasure. Rather, being a pirate is about being aware of your organizational environment as a system. A captain must be aware of the wind and the sea, the tides and the waves, the needs of the crew and the needs of the queen, and the rules of power and change. Every element is connected in the world of a pirate.

Imagine for a moment that you are captain of a pirate ship at full sail, navigating across open water under a starry sky, seeking direction. You check the night's constellations, you read the waves, and you test the wind. Now, you look at your map. You know that the two-dimensional map before you is an imperfect representation of a multidimensional planet. The map might suggest that each ocean is a separate entity, but you know that all water on the planet is connected. You know that the land masses drawn on the map are only approximations of their true size and shape. And you know that the edges of the map marked *there be monsters here* are not to be avoided, but are unexplored realms of opportunity. You have faith that you won't sail off the edge of the map.

This book is like that map: a flat view of an intricate, interconnected world. Try reading it the way you would read a map. You are at one point on the map and want to move through a real-world landscape—or waterscape—to another location. You know that you need your compass to give you direction, the stars to guide you, and the map to give you a sense of how your current location is connected to your future location. These tools of career and life navigation are explored in this book through the eyes of a pirate using a variety of guiding principles to chart a course.

As we began applying pirate wisdom principles in our lives, we found ourselves moving further and further away from trusting guides that lead straightaway to some destination or up some ladder. We put away the maps and the ladder. We realized that on our ships, we have to steer by the stars, the wind, the tide, and, most importantly, our sense of self and our values. We are sailing under the flag of possibility across the great sea of destiny, in search of adventure.

Chapter 3

The Pirate Wisdom Code

The Lesson of Political Savvy

Pirates use political savvy to make a good living and a good life.

There is no organization in which we can avoid politics. Every organization has some sort of internal political structure that determines how decisions are made and work gets done. Organizational politics are often marked by power schmoozing, self-promotion, rumor mills, jockeying for resources, and insider cliques. At their worst, politics become a world of secret deal making, relationship superseding performance, or dirty backroom negotiations: "You help me get the board's approval for this proposal, and I'll put your building renovation on the top of the list." Even in organizations untouched by dirty deals, many people feel trapped in everyday webs of politics, power, and bureaucratic control, like characters in a Dilbert comic strip.

The reality is that the workplace, like any locus of group interaction, is driven by people and relationships. Organizational politics are about dealing with myriad interactions that occur when people with widely varying backgrounds, agendas, and personalities come together and try to get something done. Frustration, stress, and feelings of ineffectiveness can stem from being unable to manage the political dynamics of our organizations. Yet situations with political implications are inevitable parts of our everyday world. Here are a few examples:

- We need to start a new project, so we have to sell the idea to management, get appropriate permissions, identify our resources, get our talent in place, broker partnerships, motivate our team to meet deadlines, and deal with outside agencies. Each of these steps is political and requires knowing how to deal with the specific political ecosystem of our organization.

- We need information. Simple information. But the act of getting one piece of seemingly simple information may call for significant political prowess. Say we are writing a grant application that asks for the demographics of our market. Do we try to get the information from institutional research, the resource development office, marketing, or customer service? What are the ramifications of approaching each of these potential sources? Which will require lengthy approvals? Who might feel threatened that we are planning a project that overlaps with their area? Who might raise a ruckus in response to a perceived encroachment or try to step in and take over our project? We need to know where to get the data quickly without triggering some unforeseen response. Information, even simple information, is power.

- We need someone to proofread a report that is due tomorrow. But this report reveals details of our budget and several sensitive decisions we are proposing. Who can we trust to keep a secret from folks who might resist our plans before we have time to sell them, or blindside us with attacks on our ideas in an upcoming meeting?

Some clues that you may be facing a potential political predicament emerge when you find yourself asking questions like:

- *Why did they get so upset at such a simple request?*
- *Why did they go the president (or vice president or director) with their concerns about my plans instead of coming to me?*
- *If they needed my help, why didn't they just ask?*

Yes, you know how this works. Yes, you can deal with the quagmire or sandbar or blockade. But aren't you sick of the old games? What we're suggesting is a new approach, a pirate wisdom approach to maneuvering political waters that can help you be more effective and less frustrated.

Political savvy is about how to motivate and move individuals and groups of people to get the work done, whatever the work. Politically savvy pirates navigate systems, rules, politics, and paradigms. As pirates look around inside their organization, they figure out the cultural ecosystem operating beneath the seemingly disconnected sets of instructions, policies, procedures, practices, and people. Just as a good sailor recognizes the dynamic interplay between the ocean of air above and the ocean of water below his ship, the good pirate recognizes the interaction among elements in his organizational environment. Pirates react to patterns of people and behaviors in the organization rather than to individuals or incidents, much like a master chess player studies an opponent's moves and responds to the pattern, not to a single move. And pirates know how to have fun along the way.

The Lesson of Destiny

Pirates radically embrace their destiny.

The word *destiny* is a sailor's term; it has to do with aligning your ship with nothing earthbound, with pointing yourself in the direction of the stars. Pirates know that every moment is rich with information sent by destiny to guide them, and they steer by nonphysical markers. Pirates see the world as miraculous rather than threatening, serendipitous rather than capricious. This perspective keeps them from letting the part of them that is afraid make their decisions. Pirates never let their fears steer the ship. Rather than resisting what life brings them, pirates are astonished by nothing and find wonder in everything.

The Lesson of Energy

Pirates bring positive energy to their work and to people around them.

Pirates know how to have a good time while managing the politics around them and getting their work done. In fact, pirates believe that happiness is a prime purpose of life, and that work doesn't have to be unpleasant or stressful to be effective. Maybe your reaction is, "Well, that's easy to say. But you don't know my job or the pressure I'm under!" The breed of pirates with which we deal would reply, "Arrr! It seems simple, matey: If ye be glad with yer work, fair winds to ye. If yer business makes ye hang the jib, then ye be a squiffy landlubber indeed!"

In fact, pirates don't waste time judging what should or shouldn't make someone else happy. But they do list toward the optimistic side of the ship. They tend to agree with Joan Duncan Oliver, author of *Happiness*, who claims, "Our best hope of having a good life...is to develop the kindlier, friendlier, more optimistic side of our nature." Pirates may not always be the gentlest of folks, but they do cultivate a positive work environment for themselves and others. At their best, pirates know that work (and life) is about living your gifts, fully and in the present. They know that workplaces too often are entropic environments, squeezing life out of people in the drive for the bottom line or the executive office. They eschew the hoary Western assumption that if you look like you are having too much fun, you can't be working hard enough.

Good pirate captains are transformational leaders, balancing the organization's goals with the vitality of the individuals that make those goals happen. And they make sure their ships are buoyant with joie de vivre.

The Lesson of Workplace Politics

Workplace politics and air are all the same to pirates.

Many folks like to brag about not engaging in workplace politics. "I don't play politics," or "I don't know how to play these games," they'll say, almost as a point of pride. Since politics are so often construed as dirty, many good leaders feel that being apolitical or politically naïve keeps them clean and even makes them better leaders and people. But pirates know that politics are not necessarily dirty and political players are not all crooked. Organizational relationships and politics are synonymous. Politics are essentially the negotiation of relationships, and relationships are only dirty if you sully them. We get to choose. In fact, every human advancement in the developed world—from Stonehenge to the fall of the Berlin wall to eBay—required relationship management and political finesse. The world runs on relationships.

Furthermore, we contend that every organization, from a Girl Scout troop to a multimillion dollar international corporation, is rife with relationships, and therefore with politics. So don't get hung up on politics. Denying our participation in politics is a bit like saying, "Oh, I don't do air." If the air in a room is dirty, you filter it or get out of the room or you can't breathe. If you don't do politics, you either begin to suffocate in the organization or you have to leave. Learning to be a pirate gives us the ability to find the political oxygen in any system.

For a good pirate, sailing through political waters is as easy as breathing fresh open air.

The Lesson of Rules

Pirates don't break rules, they shift paradigms.

Good pirates know that the organizational ocean in which they are sailing is filled with dynamic yet interrelated sets of socially constructed and agreed upon rules, habits, customs, and shared histories. They see their organization as a product of its living and changing culture. Pirates understand that rules—the policies, procedures, acceptable standards—arise from the powerful recurrent tides of the organization's collective core beliefs about who it is, what it is trying to do, and what its environment is.

Pirates understand that an organization's rules may not tell us the most effective, efficient, or enjoyable ways to accomplish something. More often, they tell us what *not* to do and where *not* to go in order to stay within the safe bounds of the organization's current world view. Pirates may find themselves bored or constrained by the boundaries of secure, familiar waters, and eager to push to the limits. But savvy pirates are not foolish enough to risk the gallows by treading into forbidden seas or trafficking in illegal affairs. A bit of history about our piratical predecessors may shed light on how to plot a course through this dilemma.

Though romanticized in literature and movies as anarchistic rogues above all law and constraint, pirates, particularly during the Golden Age of Atlantic piracy in the 17th and early 18th centuries, often followed well established codes and standards. A common form of piracy in this era was that of the privateer, a privately owned ship (with the same designation given to its captain and crew) bearing *Letters of Marque* from the king or queen of a given country, authorizing it as a law-abiding combatant in time of war and to raid ships from other countries or to gain reparation for specified offenses in time of peace. Colonial governments active in the Caribbean (especially Spain, England, France, and Portugal) commissioned privateers to attack ships of opposing flags, granting them immunity from reprisal according to the well-known *Articles of Piracy* and rewarding privateers for their labor by allowing them to take large spoils from ships or properties they overpowered.

Privateers were often sailors who left the confines of traditional navy or merchant ships to avoid abuse and hardships. Many sailors were forced onto these ships or conscripted into service to pay off debts, and naval life was marked by brutal conditions and an oppressive social order that offered little reward and no future. The earnings and living conditions of the privateer were significantly better than that on traditional navy or merchant ships. In addition, privateers often had more crewmembers per ship, so the workload was reduced. While many were cruel in their own way, privateers and pirates treated each member of the crew relatively fairly and followed very clearly understood codes of conduct and business.

In fact, such pirate ships were some of the earliest documented examples of democratic organizations. According to pirate historian David Cordingly, "a hundred years before the French Revolution, the pirate companies were run on lines in which liberty, equality, and brotherhood were the rule rather than the exception." Everyone on the ship had an equal vote and received a specified share of the treasure. Crew members elected the captain and voted on where they would sail and whether or not they would go into battle. If the majority of the crew became dissatisfied with the performance of the captain, they could elect a new one. Before a voyage, a set of articles was drafted and signed by each member of the ship's company, outlining the distribution of shares of plunder, the code of conduct for life aboard the ship, and associated punishments for breaking the code.

Pirates even developed early disability insurance. Anyone who was injured or lost a limb or joint or eye in time of an engagement would be compensated for the loss with an amount of money specified by his ship's code. Many pirate ships imposed rules such as no smoking below decks after sunset, lights out at eight o'clock, no women or boys aboard ship, and no fighting or gambling. Pirates took care of each other, shared the wealth and decision making, and had clearly defined standards of acceptable behavior.

So, these pirate ancestors of ours shifted the paradigm, the broadly held view that defined the current reality as the relatively powerless and unsavory life of a sailor. They built their own society complete with laws and job roles and an economic system. They practiced a radical form of egalitarianism rarely seen in their world at that time and created a more liberating life on their ships for many men who had no hope or future. These pirates lived on the fringe, saw the need for change, and navigated new waters.

The Lesson of Freedom

A pirate's greatest treasure is freedom.

Why did pirates go to so much trouble to build this new democratically based paradigm? In part, it was in response to the cruelty of the royal navy—as a form of workers revolt; in part, it was to acquire wealth that was being exchanged on the merchant ships. But perhaps the most powerful motivation was the craving for liberation and freedom. Pirates value their liberty as an essential of living and do not feel at peace unless they feel free. Good pirates recognize that freedom comes at the cost of responsibility, and they are willing to pay the price to be fully alive. Pirates live by the code that Robert Louis Stevenson set out: "To know what you prefer instead of humbly saying Amen to what the world tells you you ought to prefer, is to have kept your soul alive." Our modern Hollywood pirate, Captain Jack Sparrow (*Pirates of the Caribbean*), articulates this treasuring of freedom in his description of his ship, the Black Pearl:

> *Wherever we want to go, we go.*
> *That's what a ship is, you know.*
> *It's not just a keel and hull and a deck and sails.*
> *That's what a ship needs.*
> *But what a ship is—what the Black Pearl really is—*
> *is FREEDOM!*

Chapter 4

Pirate Basics

As we began practicing pirate wisdom, we defined ourselves as pirates; our department as the ship; our team as the crew; the entire institution as the armada; the vice president, president, board, and customers as an assortment of queens (regardless of gender); and the external organizational environment as the ocean. This chapter introduces the organizational pirate metaphor and offers fundamentals about the language, the players, and rules of engagement that form the basic *how-to*s of pirate wisdom.

How to Tell if Yer a Pirate

You may not have a parrot on your shoulder, a tattoo, or an eye-patch, but if you yearn to have your hand on the wheel of your own ship, the wind in your hair, or a chest full of treasure, yer a pirate. How can you tell for sure?

- *You like to dress up and it's not Halloween.*
- *The rules only count if you made them.*
- *You are more interested in sailing a fast schooner than commanding a battleship.*

- *You wear a gold hoop earring with your Armani suit, and you are a man.*
- *You have a secret tattoo under your Armani suit, and you are a woman.*
- *You think in terms of nautical miles and degrees of latitude.*
- *The queen never points at you when she says, "Off with their heads!"*
- *By the time they realize the treasure is missing, you are already at the horizon.*

Know Yer Ship and Ocean

Every day you board your ship, which is part of the armada. Ships come in all sizes and designs for different purposes, which represent a multitude of choices and compromises. Sometimes other people try to define your ship for you, telling you that you are on an old leaky junker. You don't have to live down to their description. You may not be able to convert a battleship to a schooner, but in the political ocean, the way you sail your ship determines the type of ship you are on.

In addition, every ocean has a different personality. The Atlantic is not the Pacific or the Sea of Cortez. It is wise to choose your ship to match the ocean currents. Some oceans call for small, fast ships that can maneuver quickly but won't carry much cargo or hold up long under fire. Some oceans require large, stable vessels that, while slower, can carry a sizeable crew through rough waters. The key is to recognize what ocean you are sailing, and sail accordingly.

Know the Players

Know your queen. Every pirate has a queen. And you usually don't get to choose yours. Your queen might not be a person, but could be a board of directors, a council of trustees, a loyal set of fans, or your customers. In some instances, the real queen may not hold the title. We all know stories about the power behind the throne. Still, there is always a queen. And even the queen serves her queen.

Why a queen, you may ask? Picture Elizabeth R., the brilliant and politically astute daughter of Henry VIII, who spoke six languages and outmaneuvered the best political minds of her time. And she knew how to get pirates to work for her. For the rest of this book, when we refer to your queen, picture yourself in full pirate regalia, captain of the fastest ship in the fleet, presenting treasures to your respected queen, Elizabeth R.

It is your job to take care of your queen, because it is her job to gather, use, and protect resources. So bring her treasure. She needs to know you are loyal and respect her, so talk to her about her strengths and learn from her. If you bring her treasure but bend a few rules to do so, she might criticize you in public but continue to support you in private. Her support is of the utmost importance to you. And you are critical to her success. You need her support so that you have the freedom to steer your ship where you want to go. She needs you to bring treasure and explore new lands.

Every queen has a court. Even if you are a member of that court, you will need to attend to the dukes, princes, princesses, men-in-arms, and other captains. If you attend only to the queen, you may fall into a trap of alienating the rest of the court.

At some point in every court there is a change in power. The winds always quarter, and the tides always change. As a pirate you always must keep your nose in the wind and sense the direction the power is shifting. If you see that the queen is being replaced, you should transfer your allegiance cautiously and respectfully; never abandon the old queen before she fully hands over her crown to a successor. After a power shift, do not demonstrate too much allegiance to the old regime, or you might find yourself locked out of the castle.

If you are the queen, you will always be dealing with your court and your pirates. Go ahead and take the gifts of treasure, but be aware of who brings you gifts and why. Be even more aware of what treasures capture your eye and heart, and strive to know the hearts of those around you. It is your job to be a good queen and to help your pirates be good pirates.

Know the Crew

As a pirate captain, you assess whether your crew wants to be on a pirate ship, and if they belong on your ship in particular. Potential crewmembers need to understand the difference between sailing on a merchant ship, serving in the queen's navy, or being on your pirate ship. You have a problem if they get seasick before you ever set sail. Perhaps they belong onshore or on a different ship. It is also the captain's responsibility to make sure that crewmembers' talents and skills match their assignments on the ship. Pilots don't make good cooks.

Know Yerself

When we began exploring pirates, whether real-life or fictional, we found a range of reasons for why they got into the pirate business:

- Robin Hood was in it to make England a good and fair country.
- Sir Francis Drake, at least the Errol Flynn version, was in it to support his queen and country.
- Anne Bonny was in it to escape old bonds and traditional gender roles.
- Peter Pan did not want to grow up, and was in it for the fun.
- Captain Jack Sparrow, the playful and quirky Johnny Depp character from Pirates of the Caribbean, was in it for the freedom.
- Jimmy Buffet is the fun-loving, freewheeling Mogul of Margaritaville. A self-proclaimed "adequate musician" and "fair vocalist," he discovered early on that "rock-and-roll was like getting to be a pirate." With his pulse on America's yen for freedom, he turned the allure of island escapism into an $80 million a year business and made Key West a new-age pirate getaway. And he is still in it for the fun.

And some honorary pirates:

- Mahatma Gandhi pirated the British political system with a new form of nonviolent protest against injustice—civil disobedience—focused on bringing freedom to India. India's independence from British occupation was largely a triumph of Gandhi's human will. "My life is my message," he wrote. 'Nuff said.
- Tom Peters, the irreverent pirate of traditional management paradigms, shifted business's focus from the bottom line to corporate passion, radical change, creative disorder, and innovation. His landmark 1982 bestseller, *In Search of Excellence*, spawned a new literary genre, the popular self-help business book. His unconventional views led *Business Week* to dub him "business' best friend and worst nightmare." He rails against the status quo and dares audiences to "declare war on rules, organizational barriers, and bureaucracies." He is the self-described "prince of disorder, champion of bold failures, maestro of zest, and corporate cheerleader." A pirate if ever we've seen one.
- Oprah Winfrey pirated daytime TV with a wildly successful new format of humanistic programming and is in the pirate business to improve the

lives of millions of men and women. From humble beginnings in Mississippi, Winfrey emerged as one of the most powerful women in the world, a poster child for the American Dream. "*Live your best life,*" her corporate tagline, is a tenet any good pirate would honor.

Given this eclectic set of role models, here are some questions to consider about your core values and aspirations for becoming a pirate: What do you desire? What gets you up in the morning, what keeps you up nights, what brings out the best in you? What do you want to achieve? What legacy do you want to leave behind? Only you can know your deepest dreams and motivations. And the choice to bring them to life is yours.

Choose Yer Role

Once you know the players and your personal piratical motivations, you can determine which role will help you best achieve your goals. Will you be the queen, the pirate captain, or a member of the crew? You can be a pirate from any of these positions. You might be the pirate queen, managing a pirate fleet. Or, perhaps you are the captain of the ship, leading and caring for your crew. Or maybe you are the pilot, directing your strengths toward charting a good course and steering the ship while the captain manages the crew and queen. You might choose to be a crewmember, an active shipmate who enjoys the pirate life and shares the desire for a certain type of treasure. Any role you choose can change with the wind: Sometimes you're the queen, sometimes the captain, sometimes a sailor, and sometimes you simply are in training for your next role. It depends on the ocean at the time and depends on your strengths and your heart. In the end, it depends on what you choose.

It helps to remember that each role has associated advantages and disadvantages. You must be willing to pay the cost to reap the benefits of each position. Here's a chart that outlines the pros and cons to help you choose:

	COST	BENEFIT
Queen	• You have no privacy. • You are an easy target for attack. • You always have to dress up. • Sometimes the crown gives you a headache.	• The job pays well. • Everyone knows you're the queen. • You can yell *off with their heads*. • You can get things done.
Pirate Captain	• You have to stand outside in bad weather. • You have to recruit and train new sailors. • You have to face the risk of mutiny at sea. • Sometimes the queen (or other authorities) wants to hang you. • You make people jealous.	• You have the most influence over where you're going and how to get there. • You get to dress however you wish. • You get the first pick of the treasure. • You get to chase the horizon.
Pirate Crew	• You have only one vote toward where you're going or what battles you fight. • You have to work hard. • Ships can be dangerous places.	• You get a fair share of the treasure. • You may work hard, but you're treated better than the queen's navy. • You get to taste adventure.

Keep a Captain's Log

Whichever role you are playing, it helps to keep a close monitor on how well you are doing to ascertain whether you truly are functioning as a good queen or pirate or crew member. The challenge is to steer clear of the Bermuda Triangle of self-deception. Self-deception can undermine our performance by blinding us to the reality of situations and our roles in them, leading us to choices that make matters worse. Unaware, we can get drawn into powerful vortexes of self-justification or inappropriate blame and begin to believe some self-made illusion of reality. Because sailing is challenging enough, avoiding anything that clouds discernment is crucial for a pirate.

A captain's log has proven to be a powerful tool to keep us honest with ourselves. We have found that scrupulous, regular self-reflection is one way of monitoring how well we are following our internal compass. We ask ourselves:

1. *How happy am I? How happy is my crew?*
2. *How effective am I in meeting my goals and getting my treasure?*
3. *Am I acting in alignment with my personal values?*
4. *Is my ship in alignment with my personal values?*

As we do our appraisal in each of these areas, we strive to avoid letting ourselves get by with easy answers. We ask the harder follow-up probe, "How do I know?" to each question. And we ask for feedback from others. We are not trying to make everyone happy, but we listen for patterns of responses that point to an off-course decision or blind spot in our character or actions. This exercise fine tunes our intuition and helps develop an inner resiliency that gets us through dark days and rough waters.

Reading the Map

In the same way that pirates develop skills at monitoring their internal compass, they need to skillfully navigate by cues in the external environment. Political markers are sometimes unclear or absent altogether. On open seas, pirates must navigate by stars, winds, the colors of the water, lighthouses, experience, and input from other sailors. New waters may have low visibility or hidden reefs and call for careful scrutiny before going full sail ahead. Inexperienced pirates can miss subtle landmarks. There is a myth that good sailors are born, not bred, but even if sailing is not in your blood, you can learn good navigational skills. Success comes from avoiding obstacles you can predict and developing the buoyancy and confidence to handle those you cannot avoid. You can learn to be a pirate.

Hunting for Treasure

> *Gold won't satisfy the desire for freedom.*
> *Fame won't satisfy the desire for love.*

Treasure comes in many forms. As the pirate Captain Jack Sparrow argues, "Not all treasure is silver and gold, mate." (*Pirates of the Caribbean*). Everyone wants some sort of treasure, be it prestige, title, power, freedom, adventure, fortune, glory, security, freedom to be creative, the satisfaction of helping others, or advancement of a personal cause. If you are to be an effective pirate, now's the time to come clean about your treasure.

Close the door, get ready to destroy the evidence, and for once, answer just for yourself: *What do you really, truly want?*
And, how much of it will it take to satisfy you?
So...just imagine you've got treasure.
What is it?
Gold?...How much?
Power?...What would you do with it?
Title?...Which one do you want?
Fame?...Will the keys to the city suffice, or do you need the Nobel prize?
Freedom?...To do what?
Security?...What will make you feel secure?...And for how long?
Want to make a difference in the world?...Where? For whom? In what way?
And how far are you willing to go to get what you truly want?

We believe you cannot be a wise pirate if you don't know what your pirating is about. The thing about pirates is that there can be absolutely NO judgment about the type of treasure one seeks. Why chase notoriety when what you really want is serenity? And there is no sin in admitting you want gold, and lots of it.

Just get clear about your pirating.

You can seek as many treasures as you like, but you will never be satisfied if you are chasing the wrong treasure.

Enjoy Yer Treasure

Good pirates know how to enjoy their treasure. They enjoy getting it as much as they enjoy having it. Ebenezer Scrooge was a bad pirate. He had all the treasure, but he never enjoyed it.

Jimmy Buffet says he enjoys every minute of amassing his treasure. He seems surprised that his music has made him rich. He just wanted to be free, to make a little music, and to make people laugh. For nearly three decades, his concerts have had record-breaking attendance. And he is still having fun.

Pirates may be serious about treasure, but they do not have to be serious to get it. The key is to enjoy every bit you get. And pirates can have many kinds of treasures: They do not have to choose between power and love, between success and fun, between the satisfaction of achievement and the joy of the journey. Pirates can have it all.

Hoist the Jolly Roger

Pirates are great actors, and they stage their own plays. When meeting adversaries or critics, pirates sometimes take on the roles they have been criticized for playing and boldly embody their opponents' worst nightmares. Other times, they shock challengers with an unexpectedly conciliatory response. This gives the pirate the opportunity to build political alliances that can advance everyone toward their personal treasure. Sometimes pirates simply entertain themselves and have fun taking on some eccentric role they decide to play today. Here are some secrets from our treasure chest about staging your own pirate play:

1. Dress the part when you play the part. If you are the captain, your crew likes to see you dress like a pirate. They look for the flash and the edginess of rebellion when you walk by them. That gives them courage.

2. Dress for your queen when you go to court. But don't try to blend in with everyone or hide the fact that you're a pirate. Aim for pirate chic—sharp, well-groomed, put together—but retain your roguish edge.

3. Dress to send the message you intend. Pirates are sticklers for impression, even down to the shoes. Each morning, a pirate has a little fun as she considers her costume:

   Who am I and my ship meeting today?

   Is this a light-colored day? Or do I need electric blue? Or maybe black?

   Flats? Heels? Boots? Stilettos?

   Wool? Leather? Silk? Chains?

   The gold hoop or the diamond stud?

HOW TO DRESS LIKE A PIRATE	
Male:	Female:
• perfect coif	• a barely constrained wild mane
• impeccably cut suit with a hint of flair	• no department store standards
• subtlest gold earring	• unique pieces assembled in eclectic montage
• an odd love of boots	• a flash of gold, sparkle, or a daring cut

A different level of consideration must be made in times of challenge. At such times, you must consider whether to dress as the Jolly Roger, offering your adversaries an invitation to surrender and be treated well, or as the Red Flag, offering no quarter, saying to all you meet, "Surrender will not be accepted today." And you use your battle flags as a way of dressing not only yourself, but also your ship, to convey your desired message. Hoisting the Jolly Roger sends the message that you mean serious business, but you are willing to negotiate concessions. Sporting the Red Flag sends the unmistakable message that a fight is imminent, and no compromise will be brooked, so this dress is used very sparingly. Most people want to avoid a fight and so will respond to the Jolly Roger and come to the bargaining table. By hoisting the Jolly Roger, you display the vivid fact that *you* are in control of the situation. When your power sails before you, you meet little resistance.

One warning: It is dangerous to raise the Red Flag and play the angry pirate role unless you are fully in charge of your communications and emotions. If you lose your temper, you might lose your head or your ship. You can use anger effectively, but do not let anger use you.

Aim for Madness or Brilliance

<u>Will Turner:</u>   *This is either madness...or brilliance.*

<u>Jack Sparrow:</u>   *It's remarkable how often those two traits coincide.*

—Pirates of the Caribbean: The Curse of the Black Pearl

Pirating has much to do with reputation. An effective way to cultivate a piratical reputation is to attract attention with your seeming madness. Let them think you are crazy or foolish while you are assessing the situation and making sense out of complex alternatives and relationships. Then when you act, those around you will be startled by how far ahead of the game you are. Yeah, you're mad—mad like a coyote.

When the pirate Jack Sparrow encounters Commodore Norrington on the dock in Port Royal, the commodore recognizes him by name and reputation but finds his weapons and personal effects to be laughably lacking. "No additional shot or powder, a compass that doesn't point north...You are undoubtedly the worst pirate I've ever heard of." Undaunted, Sparrow counters, "But you *have* heard of me."

Don't try to fit the standard script. As a pirate, you are an artist, and you see the world differently. Therefore you act differently, not for the sake of being different, but for the personal joy and the power of being brilliant. Hold your head high, take a risk, and do something distinctive or outrageous. If you have an important presentation to give, abandon the mundane PowerPoint and bring your message to life with a field trip or interactive production. Don't plan another fundraising dinner with the predictable guest speaker; throw a costume ball or rock concert. Don't hold another boring meeting; host a theme party. Don't send a memo, send a singing telegram. Not every action should be equally untamed, or your wildness will become predictable, but let your creativity flow and your brilliance shine.

If you do not feel talented or creative, you can surround yourself with nontraditional, imaginative people, and their creative spirits will stimulate yours. Management and innovation guru Tom Peters reminds us that we become who we hang out with, and he suggests that we hire "crazies" and "freaks"—unconventional thinkers who promote weirdness and innovation (and, he says, the *only* ones who truly succeed)—and that we turn them loose to do something "insanely great."

We believe that every pirate has a creative spirit lurking inside. Yours may not be the painter, singer, dancer sort of spirit, but trust that the artist is in there. You are fueled by the creative force of the universe, and you can express this creativity any way you choose. As a pirate, you feel this essential life force pumping through your veins with the generative energy to guide you to your treasure. Listen for that voice inside that you may have ignored until it has become a whisper. Feel the stirring of your inner creative power, and then begin to let it out in your own brilliant or madcap way. As Isabel Allende so beautifully suggests, "You are the storyteller of your own life, and you can create your own legend or not." At the very least, entertain yourself.

Make Yer Weakness Yer Strength

> *The greatest weakness of all is the great fear of appearing weak.*
> —Jacques Benigne Bossuel

Know your personal strengths and weaknesses. Build your crew to fill in the gaps in your knowledge, skills, and abilities so you always play to your strengths and at the same time admit to your weaknesses. Don't be caught by the illusion that you'll be stronger by masking your weak spots. Know them. Own them. And surround yourself by crewmembers who can do what you can't do well and who know what you don't know.

In fact, you can capitalize on seeming weaknesses by calling attention to them. If you don't spell well, for example, point it out immediately: "My mind moves faster than my speller, so I'll need your help as we move through these ideas." This way, rather than letting this minor imperfection become a mark by which others disparage you and your work, you've subtly recast your weakness as trivia. In the end, your weakness becomes your strength. What you gain by highlighting your flaw so offhandedly is to disarm potential critics and direct attention where you want it: on your assets. You come off looking like a self-confident global thinker with a sense of humor.

Remember the famous pirate, Sherlock Holmes? He admitted that he did not know all the facts, but needed only to know where to find them: "A man should keep his little brain attic stocked with all the furniture that he is likely to use, and the rest he can put away in the lumber room of his library, where he can get it if he wants it."

Another master of self-definition was Elizabeth R., the piratical queen of England who excelled at politics and war as well as any man and led her impoverished, disjointed country into an age of power and prosperity. Known for her unorthodox ways, she would flaunt her small size and feminine weakness by riding onto the battlefield in ill-fitting oversized amour on a white horse.

Set Yer Own Rules

> *Rules are for people who don't know what to do.*
> *Trails are for people who are lost.*

Every organization has existing rules that define its winners and losers. Pirates don't thrive in the win-lose environment, because they are by definition *outsiders* and destined to lose. Pirates have no interest in playing a game in which they are preordained as losers, so they establish their own rules of play. Pirates also see the weakness in compromising oneself to harmonize with the established order, like barking out orders because they are barked at you or garnishing your office with roses because these are the boss's favorite.

How do you create your own rules? At the most extreme end of the scale, since pirates live large, you can start by becoming what we call a Paradigm Pirate. To pirate a paradigm—the fundamental belief system driving whatever game is being played—you do not just change the rules, you change the entire game. Although we agree that *paradigm shift* is an overused term in the business world, as pirates, we think this notion of prompting radical changes in the unquestioned set of beliefs, theories, or thought patterns that underlie complex systems or organizations is a concept worth pursuing.

This book is based on challenging the standard truths. We redefine pirates as good guys and politics as relationships. We say work should and can be fun. We say you do not have to wait until you retire to have a life. We say that money is not the only way to keep score or the only treasure to seek. The old patterns of business and organizational management are not working for us or for many people we know, so we suggest an alternative. If your paradigm, or whatever you want to call it, does not work for you, the pirate says, "Change it!" Change the rules of engagement, and you change the game.

That is exactly what the New England Patriots did in professional football. When salary caps made it hard to recruit big-name proven champions, they changed to a strategy of assembling a stable of strong young players with more potential than star power. They used a game strategy that was more about teamwork and collaboration than grandstanding by one or two players. And it worked. And other teams followed their lead.

Nike did the same thing. It changed the running-shoe marketing game by focusing not on the quality of the shoe, but on the emotional connection to running, especially for women. Nike said, "Just do it!" and the world took up the challenge.

If you want to get serious about pirating the existing world view of your organization, you might start with the recommendation of paradigm man Joel Barker and look at the edges of your industry. Ask yourself, "If I could do one thing that could change the nature of my workplace or industry for the better, what would I do?" Barker argues that the edges—what he calls the "verges"—of our social and economic worlds are the places where things that are different intersect and opportunity lurks. It is in these dynamic intersections that pirates are comfortable and find fertile ground for shaping their own futures.

A few ground rules for paradigm piracy:

- *Don't mess with the forces of nature.*
- *Define a new formula within the unmovable boundaries.*
- *Set the rules to move you and your crew toward treasure.*
- *Always act like you know what you're doing.*

Sometimes you can advance your desired outcomes by pirating the rules on a smaller scale. As a pirate, if you are called in to give a presentation on your department's outcomes, you are savvy enough to know that this might be more than a friendly review with kudos waiting at the end of the line. This is time to take the helm. You give them what they ask for, but not in the way they expect. Perhaps one of your teams is making magical strides but not getting much notice, or you have a killer idea for a new client group that is getting no movement from the marketing division. This is the opportunity to tell your queen what you want her to know, the way you want her to know it. But remember, the queen and court (*i.e.*, the cultural establishment) value and validate ideas that are familiar or dear to them, so be sure to wrap your message in a package they will respond to, whether it's meeting one of their strategic agendas, besting a particular competitor that is plaguing them, or bringing home the jewels from a new shore. Whatever the situation, the person who writes the rules has control over the outcomes. Make sure you are that person.

> *You can and should shape your own future,*
> *because if you don't someone else surely will.*
> —Joel Barker

Hold Yer Line

Changing the rules doesn't mean breaking the rules or operating outside the bounds of integrity. As a pirate, you must know your queen's rules about right and wrong in order to keep your head. At the same time, you must keep your own ethical compass. If your queen takes you too far afield of your moral boundaries and expects you to cross that line, it might be time to find a new queen. There is always another queen.

Once you cross the line, you will be unable to compute right and wrong. What's the difference between a little cheating and a little bit more? The next thing you know, you are in a corporate scandal. There is a difference between changing the rules and breaking moral codes. Good pirates don't break the code. The New England Patriots changed the rules of play in professional football, but they did not cheat.

Keep your compass calibrated with feedback from good friends in many ports. Your moral compass defines which ship you should be sailing on, which direction you should be heading, and how you captain your ship. If anything else is guiding you, then woe be unto you, mate!

Chapter 5

Leading The Crew

Keep Yer Crew Hardy

Smooth sailing through political waters is like sailing rough seas with a well-seasoned crew. Everyone on the vessel moves with the rocking of the boat and shifts with the wind. They do not need to be told in hierarchical order to go to starboard or port; they just feel the shift that is needed, and they move. The captain yells, "Tacking!" and the crew all reorganize themselves and their duties, instantly and instinctively. They don't need to be told, "Betty, pull that line," "George, handle that sheet," "Maria, close the hatches." They self-organize as the situation demands.

Ships cannot afford to hire specialists who only do one job. The same crew that sails against the wind knows how to sail with the wind. The crew that mans the sails also goes into battle and then takes the ship to dry dock and scrapes off the barnacles. An effective crew is able to adapt, without being told, to changing situations and environments.

Good pirate captains know that a well-run ship might look a little unruly at times, but that micromanaging the crew actually creates more chaos. They know that the best way to run a ship is to set a clear course and allow the crew to determine, based on individual and collective strengths, how best to get there. The crew knows success is measured by how well they advance the ship's goals and how closely their actions align with the ship's values. Captains who mandate little details never get the big results.

Managing By Pirating Around

One way to monitor the crew's progress and the overall health of the ship is to practice *Managing By Pirating Around* (MBPA). With a tip of the tricorn to Tom Peters' and Robert Waterman's (*In Search of Excellence*) popularization of the Management By Wandering Around success of such companies as Hewlett-Packard and GE, we believe this tactic is just as valid more than 20 years later, with a bit of piratical advice added for spice.

Good pirate captains keep track of what is happening on every deck, berth, hatch, and mast of the ship by being visible and present. MBPA sends a clear message that the captain is engaged and paying attention to the daily life of the ship. It provides the chance to spontaneously interact with everyone on the ship at one time or another and to learn more about their interests, passions, values, and personalities.

MBPA is undertaken with the approach of a coach or mentor rather than an inspector. Pirating around is not about snooping or striving to catch people doing things wrong. Good captains try to find out what is working right as well as what needs improving. They strive to be open and responsive and to listen without making judgments. MBPA offers gifts of serendipity for chance encounters, fortuitous problem solving, and on-the-spot professional development—such as teaching someone the easiest way to tie a bowline knot or trim a sail—while nurturing relationships that build a strong crew.

Create a Community of Power

Pirates create a community of power by helping every member of their crew be powerful. When the crew is functioning optimally—all members taking responsibility, making appropriate decisions, making things work for the good of the ship—the captain is free to chart the course and locate new treasure.

As we began trying to develop communities of power, we found it helped to contrast the activities, roles, and scenarios that characterize communities of distrust with those of ideal communities of power.

	COMMUNITY OF POWER	COMMUNITY OF DISTRUST
Mental model	• Abundance consciousness	• Zero-sum mentality
Everyday activities	• Everyone is on task, knows what the job is, and does it. • Crew helps one other. • Focus is on continuous improvement and fun.	• Everyone is fearful of being caught off task. • Everyone is a competitor. • Focus on getting mine and blocking yours.
Who does what	• Title doesn't define the role; duties shift to meet needs.	• Functions defined by title; no job description boundary crossing.
When change happens or problems arise	• Crew works together and adapts to meet the need. • Crew experiments with new ideas to solve the new problems.	• People wait to be told what to do. • People repeat same behaviors regardless of changing situation.
What the Captain does	• Grows, motivates, and inspires the crew • Catches crew doing things right	• Direct, monitors, criticizes the crew • Catches crew doing things wrong
When Captain is gone	• Work goes on. • Quality remains constant. • Crew steps up to take over.	• Work stops. • Quality drops. • Crew celebrates.
What it feels like to be the Captain	• Proud of crew and ship • No concern for the ship's long-term success • Spends time nurturing creative passions and fun	• Wary of being exploited or manipulated • Can't go on vacation without worrying • Overwhelmed, overworked, underappreciated

We envision a community of power to respond and care for each other and the captain like the crew of Captain Jack Sparrow in *Pirates of the Caribbean*. As

Jack is leaving the ship to save the governor's daughter, his crew called out to him, "What do we do if you don't come back, Captain?" He replies, "Stay to the Code," referring to the rule of *them what's left behind, stays behind.* But when Jack does not return as planned and his crew realizes that he is in danger, they risk fortune and safety to rescue him. A community of power makes sense of the pirate's code of *All for one, and one for all!*

Be the Common Vision

When we talk about common vision we get idealistic. In a community of distrust, common vision means, "I write the vision, share it with you, and now we have shared vision." One of the best examples we know of common vision emanating from a community of power was written by our founding fathers and began, "We the people of the United States, in order to form a more perfect Union…" In many ways, the fathers of our country were classic pirates. They were men of remarkable foresight and public-spiritedness who followed their personal moral compasses, successfully led loosely organized militia groups, and helped create a democratic community of power. They changed the paradigm of the times and led a new country in defining its treasure of freedom, and did so in the face of great resistance.

The first step toward forging a common vision is to find out what inspires your crew, what galvanizes them, and what they dream about. You must find out what your ship is about, what treasure this crew is seeking, why they signed onboard, and how you can merge those dreams and good intentions into a common shared vision.

Common vision does not mean that everyone wants exactly the same thing. But the vision must be big enough to hold each individual's personal aspiration. And this *Big What* must be made inarguably and indelibly clear. An extraordinary pirate captain makes the crew hungry for the Big What and becomes the archetype of the common vision. Like the Pope or the Dalai Lama, this ever-present embodiment of the vision becomes a walking, living, breathing reality rather than a strategic plan or a plaque on the wall.

Be the Leader Yer Crew Believes In

A captain worth following must give the crew an image of a leader with whom they can make an emotional connection, but someone powerful enough that they will want to follow as moonglade hugs the horizon. The pirate captain must inspire mystery, admiration, and loyalty from the crew by behaving as a powerful leader but never a dictator.

As a pirate, you must be a leader. This is the one that role that you cannot avoid, the one job duty that you cannot shirk. As leaders, you can never underestimate the energetic effect of your position. Your bad mood can set the ship adrift; your fear is more contagious than yellow fever; your smile can keep an injured seaman in the fight. You never get the luxury of blowing a gasket on deck or throwing a tantrum, unless you are alone in your cabin. Occasionally, if a crewmember is making your blood boil, you might bark, "Get out o' me eyes!" before you feel the need to bite. But you must always exude an aura of strength and self-possession.

And a funny thing happens when you act like the leader. People join your play, they act along with you. It isn't really so lonely at top for the good pirate captain. It is only lonely at the top if you climbed over everyone's dead body to get there.

Just as people yearn for higher purpose, they seek out leaders to believe in. Live up to their faith in you. Be warned, however: You must never trade being respected for being liked. If you make such a slim bargain, you will squander your influence and find yourself deserted and powerless. You abandon yourself when you seek yourself in the reflection of others.

Developing the Crew

> *There is more in us than we know.*
> *If we can be made to see it, we will be unwilling to settle for less.*
> —Kurt Hahn

Every crew needs to know that they can survive whatever challenges the seas may bring. Outward Bound is an outdoor adventure-based education program based on this principle. Its originator, Kurt Hahn, was commissioned during World War II by the British Royal Navy to help with a surprising loss of sailors when a ship went down in the North Seas before help could arrive. The strange part was that the survivors were almost all older seamen, while the younger twentysomething sailors, who were thought to be more fit and hearty and have the best odds for survival, were perishing in higher numbers. What Hahn concluded was that the older sailors were surviving because they had survived other life challenges. They knew they could make it through this challenge because they had made it through others before. Hahn concluded that living through a crisis makes us stronger and more likely to survive another one. Our abilities are largely perceptual, he believed, and by stretching past our personal perceptions of our limitations, we expand not only our abilities, but also our confidence and self-efficacy. Hahn's program to teach young British sailors self-reliance for survival during World War II became the foundation for the challenging, adventurous outdoor experiential body-mind-spirit approach to self-development that we know as Outward Bound.

Outward bound is in fact a nautical term to describe a ship leaving the safety of its harbor to head for the open seas. Outward Bound training has a saying: "If you can't get out of it, get into it." This means that to prevail in a difficult situation, you sometimes need to do what seems counterintuitive. Hiking down a steep slope, you are safer if you lean *back* into the mountain. If you are riding a runaway horse, you get it to stop by leaning back. If you go into a spin when driving on an icy road, you need to turn *into* the skid to stop the spin and keep your foot off the brake. Sometimes you have to move toward the challenge rather than away from it.

As a pirate captain, how can you treat the challenges and crises on your ship as Outward Bound training exercises? Begin by teaching your crew that they can deal with whatever difficulties come. Give them hands-on opportunities to build self-esteem and self-reliance through calculated risk taking. Let them face some Outward Bound moments and use their skills to survive.

Next, model the art of leaning into the challenge. A good pirate knows she must sometimes act counterintuitively and do the opposite of what feels natural. Make plans to hire new crewmembers with an eye for strategic growth, even while you are cutting the budget. If the budget is being slashed and your crew is deserting under the relentless do-more-with-less pressure, a natural leadership response might be to attack the defectors with *Where were you?* or *How could you?* Instead, take personal responsibility for the breakdown, and ask crewmembers how to recoup the loss and get back on board.

Developing your crew is essentially the art of seeing more in them than they see in themselves. Go beyond empowering—an overused word, yet a rarely enacted concept—and facilitate true development of your crew. Help them shift the locus of their power from external to internal sources. Empowering suggests a hierarchical granting of power from you, the empowerer, to your crew. Development suggests that you provide the environment, the resources, and the sea of possibility in which crewmembers can achieve the extraordinary and expand their belief in their own potential. Give your crew opportunities to reach higher, push harder, go further than they ever thought possible. Let them take risks in forgiving circumstances so they can learn as humans learn best, by making mistakes and learning from them. Wake them up to their personal power, and they will learn to lead themselves.

Share the Booty

Greed is the ruin of a good pirate and the wreck of a ship. If you permit greed on your ship, it will become your prison. Treasure can be a potent charm, with the power to entrap and lead your ship into perilous waters. If the hankering for *more* gets a toehold on your ship, its grasping tendrils can choke a heart, put blinders over the best lookout's eyes, and pit sailor against sailor. It spreads seeds of savagery and suspicion and can splinter your ship faster than the rockiest shoals.

Many good sailors have been snared by the *velvet chains* of their jobs, as they give more and more to keep following the mirage of their elusive treasure: "I can't take time off," they tell their families, "this deadline is too important." Or, clasping on the golden handcuffs, they say to themselves, "I can stick this out for six more years; then I'll be eligible for a partial retirement." Or they become enchanted by the treasure's gleam and will step over anyone to get more.

That which you desire beyond reason or control will hijack your life and your ship. So, never allow the demon GREED aboard your ship. Successful pirates take only what they truly need in the moment. They live with a lusty trust in the abundance of life and know there is more where that came from. They know that the more they give away, the more will come to them. They know that the rules of sharing the treasure are simple:

1. Everyone on the pirate ship gets a share of any treasure, down to the deckhand and cabin boy.
2. Share the wealth, no matter what form it takes: gold, fortune, glory, adventure, or fame.
3. Never hoard the credit for success. It is a false prize.

Giving credit away is a powerful pirating tool. If you try to keep credit and build up a credit trove, it will weigh you down with self-importance and make you an easy mark for mutiny. Instead, give credit away instantly, and always recognize and acknowledge your crew for any success the ship enjoys. Use the language of *we* to describe victories; use the language of *I* for shortfalls. This will instill a sense of pride and loyalty among the crew and teach them to be generous with each other. Model the spirit of altruism and ensure that others follow your lead. Never allow a crewmember to take advantage of another. The strongest ship is built on a framework of sharing.

When others accuse you of being territorial or greedy, they are giving you the cue to distrust them. They are revealing themselves and their motivations in their accusations, and they are bringing their own envy or deficiency of beliefs into play. Do not be seduced into playing the zero-sum game with them. Scarcity is an illusion.

Pirates sail in a sea of abundance and believe that somehow there will always be enough to go around. They recognize that scarcity is a result of people panicking and hoarding resources. Pirates also know that abundance calls for monitoring the flow of resources on and off the ship. Judicious practice means that you take only what you need and make sure that others do the same. There may be times that you have to pull the crew together to conserve while you find or create new sources. But with good leadership, the ship will provide the means to meet the needs of everyone aboard.

Never Fight on the Ship

> *No Striking one another on Board, but every Man's Quarrels to be ended on Shore, at Sword and Pistol.*
> —Pirate's Code, 1895

Pirates never let others know if there is discord among the crew. A good crew respects the image of the ship, particularly in public. Sailing under the queen's flag protects the ship, and dissension destroys the power of the flag. If the crew needs to fight, the captain takes them somewhere off the ship to a place where they can safely vent their differences. Beyond direct combat, public disputes and private rumor mills create the largest leaks in any ship. The crew must crew must stay to the code to keep the ship tight and seaworthy.

In the same vein, the captain must follow the rule to discipline in private, and praise in public. A crew will never trust a captain who humiliates or discredits them in front of their peers. The captain's goal is to promote the crew's camaraderie as that of Brethren of the Coast to keep the ship moving toward its treasure.

Crime and Punishment

Now, here's the kick: Despite the captain's best efforts, some crew members will choose to ignore good guidance and determinately find ways to rabblerouse or make life on the ship untenable for others. Occasionally, a sailor, out of sport or foolhardiness, will repeatedly put the ship into tight spots. If you detect such a pattern of behavior, you must act decisively. First, keep him close to you. Move his bunk next to yours, spend extra time with him. Talk straight with him, and tell him exactly what you see that is not working in his behavior. Make clear-cut recommendations for improvement, and document your expectations and his responses. He may not admit to or change his seditious ways, but you should give him the chance to improve under your eagle eye.

If the troublemaker won't mend his ways after all your efforts, you must make a decision. When a crew member becomes toxic to the rest of the crew, risks your safe port with the queen, or undermines your authority as captain, there is no doubt that he cannot be trusted and must go. He has broken the code and put the ship in danger, and you must ensure that he is kept beyond the reach of causing more trouble. The question becomes, do you make him walk the plank or do you maroon him?

We all know the stories of pirates forcing enemies or mutineers to walk, hands tied, off the ship via a plank of wood and into Davy Jones' locker. Historians suggest that this practice was more fiction than fact and was promoted in pirate lore to enhance mystique and image. Reality is that good pirate captains don't let situations escalate to the point where such drastic measures are needed. They keep a close eye especially on new crewmembers and find out within the first voyage whether the new shipmates should be allowed back on ship again. "Feeding the fish" by forcing them off the ship in the middle of a voyage is a radical, desperate act, and almost always avoidable.

But what if you have exhausted all means to integrate a troublemaker or landlubber into your ship's life, yet she is protected by your queen or other powers? You cannot make her walk the plank or refuse her back aboard. Now what? The answer is to maroon her. Classically, traitors and wrongdoers were dropped off on a desert island and given only a pistol with one bullet and a bit of grog. They were made *Governor of a Two Palm Island* and marooned as the ship moved on.

If you are dealing with a troublemaker who is so well loved or feared that he is untouchable, then your option is to move him from the corner office to a *cornered* office away from court. Give the scurvy dog a special assignment that no one else could possibly do, but keep him away from the seat of power and away from the treasure. Give him a title and a salary and praise, but no relevancy or jurisdiction. Monitor him carefully and give him little room to maneuver. He has a choice: Stay, swim, drown, starve, or catch another ship that might sail by.

In the work world, marooning is known as *right of assignment*. Use it prudently as a last resort. Remember that it is all right to maroon someone when no other remedy works, but keelhauling and flogging is never acceptable. These abuses of power are never applied by good captains.

A note on marooning: Even good pirates can be marooned on occasion. If you find yourself at loggerheads with your queen, captain, or crew and get marooned, you have been given an enforced holiday. Rather than struggle to change the situation or fight to get back on board the ship, simply hang your hammock between the palm trees on your island and relax. Use this time to reflect on your experience, to reconnect with your sense of self, and to clarify your treasure. Then you can hitch a ride on the next ship that comes by. There is always another ship.

Down a Cup of Grog

Laughter is the shortest distance between two people and will help any job seem easier, any journey shorter. Laughter and celebration are major motivational tools that strengthen the spirit of the ship and convey a positive message and vision. People who enjoy their jobs and roles are more effective and resilient. Any job can include fun. Ships sail more effortlessly when the crew take themselves lightly.

On the pirate ships of yore, sea shanties—shipboard working songs—helped lighten the burden of hard physical labor and alleviate boredom on long voyages. On sailing ships, shanty men, the singers leading the call and response, were valued and respected for their contributions to help sailors pull together by providing rhythms by which they could synchronize efforts and make the job and the ship go faster.

Crews live in the small confines of a ship for long periods of time and become susceptible to boredom. Bored crews entertain themselves. Sometimes this entertainment is good fun or fulfilling activities. But sometimes bored crewmembers fabricate conflict or hysterics to amuse themselves or avoid scrubbing the deck. Providing appropriate recreation keeps a crew focused and out of mischief. Good pirates are never bored. They know life is a grand adventure that keeps them creative and engaged.

These changes in latitudes, changes in attitudes
Nothing remains quite the same
Through all of the islands and all of the highlands
If we couldn't laugh we would all go insane.
—Jimmy Buffett

Chapter 6

Sailing The Ship

Count Yer Doubloons

Good pirates know *everything* about *everything* on the ship. They know the budget down to the penny. They know the ship down to the nail. They know their crewmembers down to their souls. In many ways, the happy-go-lucky pirate image is only an image. Pirates may be suave, playful, and nonchalant. But a pirate's freedom does not come without cost; it is bought with knowledge and watchfulness. A distracted captain can run aground or suffer a mutiny overnight.

This does not mean that as captain you personally must monitor all decks, watch every sail, and do all the counting. But it does mean that you should surround yourself with the best crew leaders you can find and make them your teachers. If you aren't good at budgets, ensure you have the best, most trustworthy budget managers you can find. But don't just turn the budget over to them. Have them tutor you in budget and financial processes. Let them know that you trust them, but that because you are accountable for the outcomes, you will regularly review the doubloon count.

Sail in the Direction of the Strategic Plan

As captain, you may guide your ship in whatever direction best fits your float plan, your ship's outline of what treasure you seek and how you plan to get it. But you'll find the smoothest passage if you align your float plan with your queen's strategic plan before you set sail. You can do this even if her plan seems to take you away from your desired destination. Most strategic plans are broad enough to allow you to go where you want to go while generally heading your ship in the direction of the strategic plan. The idea is to determine how its aims might complement yours. Identify places in the strategic plan that map with your interests, aims, and treasure. Look at the plan with your crew in mind: What about the queen's plan might motivate them? The crew is looking for inspiration, and you can identify aspects of the strategic plan that are exciting and meaningful. One way pirates work their plans to dovetail with those of the queen is to work selectively on the strategic plan. Some of the crew may engage one portion of the strategic plan that inspires them, validating the entire ship's allegiance to the throne. Their work then serves as a shield to allow the rest of the crew to go after treasure.

A second way pirates sail in the direction of the strategic plan is to use the leeway of interpretation. Pirates are always on the lookout for alternative and creative ways to reach a destination. When the plan says go west, they never say no, but they know they can take any direction so long as they are sailing on the westward side of the map. The gift of a good pirate captain is to define the connections between personal desires and the queen's plan and make sense of these links for both the crew and the queen. Good pirates may even be able to redirect the entire armada toward their plan if they can convince the queen there is enough treasure involved.

Pirates may engage the queen's plan selectively, but they never lie to her about it, and they never undermine her plans. Even if they disagree, they show proper allegiance to the queen and support her decisions and direction. If they cannot do so, they know it is time to find a new queen.

Pirate the Dominant Language

Each court and queen has its personal language. Attorneys talk legalese, investors talk bottom line, educators talk pedagogy, manufacturers talk supply chains, athletes talk rankings, economists talk GDP, and politicians talk polls. Pirates are multilingual and cross-cultural in that they can adopt the dress, affectations, and language of their surroundings. They can take their float plan and recast it in the dominant language of the land, as reflected in the queen's strategic plan.

Say you want to invest in a program targeting the arts in a kingdom that values utilitarianism and measurable outcomes. You would be foolish to lay out a rationale that extols the creative or motivational value of art investments. Instead, you lay out your plan for the arts in terms of reaching target markets, increasing customer retention, and increasing your return on investment. You make the arts an inarguable strategic market advantage.

It seems that many people do not understand the nuances of the dominant language anyway, so they are unlikely to argue with you. When most members of the court or the queen's fleet use the language, usually they are just repeating catch phrases or mottos, much like campaign slogans. What we are suggesting is more subtle. Gift wrap your plans in the queen's language and present it to her as a treasure. You are convincing the queen and the rest of her fleet that your ship is taking the lead in promoting the strategic plan. Follow three simple steps to secure your success:

1. Make use of the dominant language.
2. Speak articulately and confidently.
3. Repeat your message frequently.

This formula works for two reasons. First, sociolinguists point out that whoever owns the language owns the conversation. By piggybacking on the dominant language, you are increasing your power. Second, there is a remarkable connection between repetition and belief. The more often people hear the same information, the more likely they are to believe it. Hence the source of many urban legends, like the one about the lady drying her poodle in the microwave. Repetition is the pathway to belief, particularly if accompanied with feeling. So when you talk about your plans or ideas, use the queen's language the way you want people to believe it...over and over and over again. This is how positive affirmations work. Make sure your entire crew adopts the same language and uses it routinely and casually. You will know you have succeeded when you hear other people using your piratical version of the language and telling your stories. When the queen tells your story as her own, you simply smile and keep sailing.

Take Responsibility

Great power resides in taking full responsibility for your actions. Even when you are not fully responsible, if you are being questioned about something in which you are involved, be ready to say, "I am completely willing to be held 100 percent accountable for anything I'm involved in." If you can't say this, check your ethics compass; it may be pointing you away from this ship or activity. Taking responsibility is a powerful tactic for defusing critics. For example, if someone throws a fit about something they assert you did wrong, take full responsibility without getting defensive and boldly reply, "I apologize if this caused you difficulty. Now what is it you need me to do to make this work?" You do not argue. You do not make excuses. You accept the feelings the other party is asserting at face value and move to solution.

Such a response deflects attack and engages the detractor in formulating a resolution to the problem he identified, but does not invite a hostile takeover. It stops the entire court from becoming aroused into a problem frenzy that leads to witch hunts and scapegoating. Taking responsibility defuses the tension in a touchy situation and preserves your power and authority.

Tacking Upwind

The only way to sail upwind is to take a zigzagging course that keeps the sails full and the ship moving. This means that sometimes the ship might appear to be moving *away* from the desired destination. You sail slightly upwind in one direction, or tack, heading sideways to but always slightly toward your goal, for a very long time. Then you turn and tack the other way. These shallow angles allow you to sail into the wind toward your goal. While you are tacking, you are never perfectly on course (*i.e.*, aimed directly at your destination) until your final tack. This is a long, slow way to sail, but it allows you to make progress against the wind without rowing.

Tacking upwind has a few hazards. For one, you must remember to turn. This sounds silly, but getting caught up in your tack and forgetting your true mark is a common mistake. If you are on a very long tack, you may begin to feel that the direction your nose points toward is where you are actually headed. Say, for example, you identify particular partners you will need to get a new project off the ground. So you tack toward partnership building. The danger is in getting so caught up in building the partnership, holding meetings, or exploring opportunities your new partner offers that you forget to tack back toward your original project goal. It is easy to confuse the tack with your true course. Make sure your crew remembers that you are on a tack and get them ready to change direction with you when the time comes.

The other danger is the actual act of tacking, when the ship must turn the bow over 90 degrees into and past the direct assault of the wind. When you come about, your crew must be ready or the swinging of the boom might knock them overboard.

Tacking can also make those in the waters around you wonder why you have suddenly changed direction. The savvy pirate uses this seemingly unexpected change of course as a strategic advantage. By tacking upwind, you can keep your crew alert and your competition guessing; all the while, you make steady progress toward your treasure, with the wind in your face.

Attend to Lighthouses and Foghorns

Lighthouses and foghorns are classic beacons or signals to aid marine navigation. They show the way in foggy waters or give warnings of barriers in the area. As a pirate captain, you find your lighthouses and foghorns in many manifestations and locations. Some are policies that warn not to pass this point. Some are buried in the oral history or legends of your institution. Some are people who offer news, guidance, and intelligence to help you make decisions and steer your ship.

People who serve as lighthouses and foghorns let you know what is going on, who does what, who knows what, and how things are working on and around your ship. They make information available and may not even know what they have shown you. They keep you from going too far over cultural barriers and legal boundaries. Lighthouses and foghorns can keep a good pirate from becoming a marauder.

Never Sail Over a Shallow Reef

A good captain will never sail over a shallow reef that would damage the hull and sink the ship. This may seem like an obvious lesson, but sometimes the shallow reefs are not clearly visible. And, more often than we might like to admit, we have caught ourselves putting captain and crew in danger by doing something blatantly stupid. We know that ignoring the rules of navigation can capsize our ship, so why would we invite such trouble? Why would we walk on the leeward side of the ship and risk getting blown overboard?

When we are busy, tired, or emotionally distracted, we run the risk of breaking the pirating rules that are easiest to keep and most dangerous to break: Don't annoy people when it is simple to keep them happy. Skirt the wrath of the most officious officers of the court. Never let your ego or emotions lead you to imprudent acts just to prove a point. Never break codes of ethics or rules of law. Always make sure the doubloons are counted correctly.

Sail Close to the Wind (Very Advanced Pirating)

When the winds quarter, they split and come at you diagonally across two sides of the ship at once. A good pirate can tell when the wind is changing and is about to quarter, and knows this is the test of leadership and the crew's ability to respond under pressure as a team. Sometimes you find yourself facing the wind of political challenge, yet needing to move quickly to seize the treasure, sneak up on a rival, or maneuver around an impending challenge. Such situations call for sailing aggressively, yet with extreme caution.

If you decide to move as quickly as possible by *sailing close to the wind*, you are taking a risk. If you steer close to the edge of the wind, the ship can harvest the most wind power to move quickly through a tough situation. But it also is easy to lose the wind altogether from this position and be left with your sails fluttering like flags and your ship dead in the water, stranded in irons.

Sailing close to the wind requires an almost intuitive steering of the ship. You cannot explain in advance what you are about to do, since you are reading the constantly shifting wind and making decisions second by second. The crew must be able to follow you with little guidance. To be successful, your crew must be in peak form, on sharpest alert, and dead quiet. They must not give away the ship's position or strategy, since you are sailing against politically charged winds. In this situation, the crew has to understand that the captain is in control, and action is not open for debate. The crewmembers need to realize that if they fail, the ship can capsize or fall off the wind completely.

So, undertake this tactic only if you have the complete trust and backing of your crew. Everyone must act in unison and respond unquestioningly, almost instinctively. Make sure your ship's culture will allow you to move this fast. Before attempting such a maneuver for a high-stakes issue, take time to prepare your crew. You will need to build them up to a point of readiness. A crew that has performed well together over time is one that can take on such a challenge. Even with a seasoned crew, you might have to tempt them into pushing their limits and taking this challenge. Plan well and sell the plan by making them feel courageous. Nothing ventured, nothing gained!

Get to Dry Dock

Even pirates need vacations.

Barnacles grow on the hull of every ship and slow the ship down. They have to be scraped off to reduce the friction and weight they add to a vessel. To remove them, a ship must go into dry dock, in which the ship is pulled up out of the water. The entire crew must help with dry docking and cleaning, and the work of everyone pulling together lightens the load and speeds the tedious work. Although dry docking is tough work, it serves as a rest for the crew, because it is change of pace and calls for using a different set of muscles. This communal work and recuperation helps shipmates build stronger bonds. A good pirate captain schedules additional time in dry dock, time for a little relaxation before heading back to sea.

Just as it gives you the chance to clean the ship, going into dry dock gives you the chance to clear your mind. Consider the time you take off as an investment rather than loss of time, since the rejuvenation and perspective you gain will make you much more effective when you set sail again. Give yourself a chance to breathe and make an accounting of things that you have let go or tasks left undone. Hang your hammock and take time to reflect about where you are in relation to your float plan.

Take an inventory: What is holding you back? Have you gotten caught up on a tack and forgotten that your current direction is not leading you toward your real treasure? Is it time for you to turn onto a different tack? Are you still happy in your current role? Is the treasure still calling you?

Chapter 7

Navigating the Waters

Know Which Rules to Break and Which to Bend

Pirates have the reputation of being rule breakers. They are not, however, foolhardy felons or outlaws. Rarely do they break rules; more often, they bend them. Rules are boundary markers, and pirates sail between the boundaries. Good pirates are strategic. They can distinguish among laws, rules, guidelines, principles, precepts, and mores. They know when to do the minimum work on an assignment and when to go full bore. They can smell when the boundaries and borderlands will be different next year. They know, if a change is on the horizon, to wait the storm out. They always follow the easy rules to the letter: *Fill out this form. Never drink on the job. Don't steal from the company.* These rules are so easy to follow that pirates would never waste energy breaking them. The only rules that pirates break are those they judge to be immoral or in conflict with their personal values or code of honor.

Build Relationships in Every Port

Pirates are expert, incessant, and natural networkers. They cast their contact nets in every sea and invest significant energy in developing and preserving relationships on and off ship. Their networks include friends, peers, business associates, political connections, and community contacts, all of whom they cultivate wherever they go. They have an easy rapport with people, and they build business connections as easily as personal ones. They recognize that relationships are fundamentally about giving and receiving and that the flow of support, information, camaraderie, and referrals goes back and forth like the tides. Someone knows something or someone you need; you have information or resources that can support them. Pirates know how to stand out in a crowd and how to make an impression that will be remembered. They also understand the laws of connection, reciprocity, and attraction:

> *Everything is connected.*
> *Giving is receiving.*
> *Like attracts like.*

To be a good pirate, you need to build your web of relationships, knowing that everyone is somehow connected. Practice giving as receiving. Give freely when asked, and do not resent the call or worry about not having enough time, money, or resources to give. Know that what you give will return not in an instant *quid pro quo* fashion, but in knowing that the quality of your relationships, your abundance, and your happiness is defined by how you show up in the world and engage with others. Reach out to those above, below, in front, behind, and beside you. And ask for help and information when you need it. Recognize your place in the Great Mandala, the infinite circle of life that connects everything in the universe. No one is beneath your camaraderie. Know who cleans the deck, who strikes the sails, and who keeps the lookout. Strive to know the names of their mates and children. You do not have to be close friends and confidants; in fact, don't assume friendship where it does not exist. But remember that everyone is deserving of friendliness. A smile and kind word makes for smooth sailing.

Give Room at the Mark

Sailing right-of-way rules call for granting another ship's call for *room at the mark*, the opportunity to maneuver when both of you approach some location at the same time. One ship holds back to allow the other time and space to make its way. This is common seafarer's courtesy, and pirates are generally courteous. Pirates are not piranhas. They do not steal one another's wind or thunder. They know there is enough power and recognition and reward on the seas to share.

The strongest pirates give room at the mark and leave their poverty mentality at the dock. They are not worried about gaining personal glory by cutting someone else out of the race. Because they are not threatened by the success of others, pirates share not only the booty, but also the opportunity for the booty. They share possibilities. It is not that pirates freely give away all ideas, information, recognition, and opportunity; they do not share the location of their own secret treasure. But successful pirates feel no need to block another ship from its own treasure hunt. A true pirate leader is not threatened by the achievements of others.

Know How Yer Enemies Sail

Sharing opportunity doesn't mean that you do not need to play smart. Occasionally, you need to manage a competitor or negotiate your way out of a confrontation. Good pirates know that if their ship is outsized, that they must outsmart, outmaneuver, and outsail a challenger. They begin by studying their challenger's patterns, which are often surprisingly predictable.

In the 1994 comedy western *Maverick*, the wisecracking gambler Bret Maverick enters a poker game in piratical fashion, announcing his intentions to "lose for the next hour," which he does. He watches the other players and learns to read their mannerisms and betting cues. At the end of the hour, he changes his strategy. He begins applying the lessons he learned, and wins famously. Maverick is not cheating; he merely has taken possession of his competitor's patterns.

The same applies in any sea, in any industry. If you observe the people around you, they will reveal their patterns. You can plan your moves based on their patterns. One way to do this is to use the illusory power of the mirror. Reflect their actions, words, and behavior patterns back to them. Your competitors often will not recognize themselves in your reflection, but will no longer resist you and your movement. You can use this technique to maneuver around people or issues and continue on to your treasure. This approach is not aimed at besting another ship, but at maintaining your free passage toward your treasure.

Be careful, because we all have patterns. Savvy pirates attend to their habits of action and do not allow themselves to become too predictable. The artistic nature of pirates helps them disrupt their natural patterns. Like good improvisational actors, they never play the scene twice.

Practice the Art of Misdirection

The truth is a powerful weapon, because most people are too weak to resist it.
—Harriet Rubin

Telling the truth is powerful, especially if it is wild. In the movie *Pirates of the Caribbean*, Captain Jack Sparrow, under the alias of Smith, is attempting to steal a ship when the guards Mullroy and Murtogg come upon him:

Mullroy: *What's your purpose in Port Royal, Mr. Smith?*

Murtogg: *Yeah, and no lies.*

Jack Sparrow: *Well, then, I confess, it is my intention to commandeer one of these ships, pick up a crew in Tortugas, raid, pillage, plunder, and otherwise pilfer my weasely black guts out.*

Murtogg: *I said no lies.*

Mullroy: *I think he's telling the truth.*

Murtogg: *If he were telling the truth, he wouldn't have told us.*

Jack Sparrow: *Unless, of course, he knew you wouldn't believe the truth even if he told it to you.*

The guards, true to form, do not believe Jack, because his truth is too wild.

Pirates always play true to their word. A classic tale of misdirection is that told by Mark Twain about Joan of Arc, the French peasant girl claiming to hear voices of the saints telling her to rescue France from the English. In Twain's version of the story, in a night march with her handful of men through enemy territory, the Maid of Orleans encounters an English officer who mistakes her for an English captain out scouting for her camp. She answers the officer's questions truthfully on every count, telling him her age, description, size of her troops, and plans for crossing the bridge in front of them. She convinces the officer to let her set fire to the bridge, and she leads her small force unchallenged through the English troops, over the bridge and to safety on the other side, setting fire to it on the way across. She keeps her head under pressure, tells simple short truths, and lets the officer's assumptions carry her and her men to safety.

Especially when under scrutiny or assault, pirates do not explain too much. Detractors will make their own assumptions, fill in the blanks, and expect behavior based on their assumptions. In fact, they will misdirect themselves. Good pirates let them.

We have found that a number of rough seas can be smoothed by gentle misdirection. You can give yourself a bit more time than you predict a task might actually take. Finishing early can make you look heroic. Similarly, be cautious about taking on more projects or duties than you can do well. Because overcommitted people are given more work on most ships, you could wind up sacrificing the quality of your outcomes or your own health. Check the membership of a group before you join so you can predict how the dynamics will work. If they are bound for failure, find another team. And if you join a work team, position yourself so that your best gifts are in service. If your talents are in marketing strategies, do not get pulled into making origami centerpieces.

Sometimes a pirate gets cornered by the queen. If you are asked to get involved in something you disdain or feel is truly bad for the ship, you can strive to make your *no* sound like a *yes* while you play for time. Suggest other partners who might want to be involved, and let them say no. Suggest that a committee might be needed to give the initiative its proper due. Ask questions to distract the queen and send her in the direction of an irresistible treasure. Keep alternatives in your pocket if you anticipate being washed into such rocky shoals.

When your moral compass is threatened, the game shifts. If you are forced into waters where someone else is playing loosely with rules or ethics that put you or your crew in danger, misdirection is no longer sufficient. It is now time to sail close to the straight and narrow. Play by the rules, and play loudly and proudly. Get out of port immediately and take your ship to sea.

Play to Their Chinks, Protect Yer Chinks

> *Thou wall, O wall, O sweet and lovely wall,*
> *Show me thy chink, to blink through with mine eye!*
> —Shakespeare, *A Midsummer Night's Dream*

Good pirates are good psychologists. They recognize people's emotional proclivities. Test your skills at pirate psychology. Ask yourself, for example, what moves your queen or first mate on a deep emotional level. What will she respond to without thought? This is not about the type of gem she likes, but what decisions she will make without knowing why, or sometimes, even that she makes them. For example, will she always support a favorite courtier because she likes the tilt of his hat and color of his eyes? Will she always move to protect that small town she comes from? Will she always send resources to the outpost she is afraid may rise up and rally against her? These are her vulnerabilities.

Our chinks in the armor are the subliminal values and biases that drive us all. Often we are blind to our deepest predispositions, and our subconscious minds are sailing our ships. This makes us particularly vulnerable to people, ideas, and situations to which we are deeply attracted or fear. The better the pirates, the more in touch they are with their own vulnerabilities. Pirates know to look to their lighthouses and enemies as mirrors who reflect their chinks in the armor back to them.

Getting in touch with latent biases—yours, your crew's, your queen's—is a potent pirate skill. Pay attention to what people move toward and away from without thought. This is a bit trickier than first meets the eye. We all have things we like and dislike more than others. In fact, if you ask about their proclivities, most people will list them for you. But our conscious biases are typically the tip of our bias icebergs. Our more acute blind spots are born from our deepest loves and deepest fears. Savvy pirates practice rigorous self-reflection and don't shy away from the good, bad, or ugly their examinations reveal. As Benjamin Franklin taught us, "There are three things extremely hard: steel, a diamond, and to know one's self."

Remember Everyone Likes to Dress Up

Pirates know that the way you look affects the way you think, feel, and act, as well as how others around you react to you. They know that people dress to fit their personal metaphors and fables. Knowing this can help you decipher how those around you see themselves, what they fear, what they want to be, what they believe in the world.

Pay attention to how other people dress. What is their favorite costume? Are they always in soft flowing frills announcing they are approachable or dreamy? Do they appear buttoned down in conservative colors with classic flair, advertising their temperance and strength? Do they flaunt avant-garde fashion, exclaiming they fear no change? Or is every day their Casual Friday, with their T-shirt and sneakers as a personal protest of the office status game? From Pigpen to Cinderella, we all play out our personal fable or metaphor.

But just as we act out our personal stories through our dress, our dress can script our actions. On graduation night in Los Angeles, we high school seniors went to Disneyland. The dress was semiformal: dresses for girls, suits for guys. Disneyland knew that if kids dressed up, they were less likely to act up. They believed in the old "clothes make the man" adage, and we did not disappoint them. We acted as good as our clothes, and we behaved ourselves like proper, if fun-seeking, young men and women.

On your ship, you set the mood by how you dress and how you encourage others to dress. Help your crew to dress like a pirate occasionally. They will like it. Besides, if everyone looks like a pirate, you can blend in when you want to. And don't miss the chance to dress in the direction toward which you are sailing. If you plan to become a captain, don a nice big hat; if you have your eye on the throne, nothing but a crown will do. Whatever costume you model, however, make sure that you look and feel composed. Let your story to the world be that, whatever you wear, you are at home in your own skin.

Beware of Mermaids and Sirens

The sea holds many things to beguile or distract a sailor: storms, giant squid, sharks, mermaids, sirens, tidal waves, and flying fish. Mermaids (or mermen) and sirens call to a pirate's desires. They call to our vulnerabilities and drag us away from our true mission. They are irresistible, and the sailor who thinks she can resist is fooling herself. Odysseus escaped the sirens by lashing himself to his ship's mast and filling his crew's ears with wax. He knew that no one could resist their call. Pay attention to the places where the sirens sing, and steel yourself as you enter those waters. If you give them your ear, you will steer your ship off mission. Their song seems so natural and innocent at first, but yielding to the siren's allure can cost you the entire ship.

One siren song that snares many hapless sailors is the crisis. Big or small, there is something addictive about a perceived emergency. Inexperienced pirates think that dashing into a crisis situation to solve the problem will make them heroes. Experienced pirates know that if you handle problems when they are small, there will be no crisis to solve. They teach their crew to watch for problems in the making and handle them before they explode.

Good pirates also resist the siren song that says that looking busy means being important. This song promotes the myth that successful leadership is directly proportional to busyness. In fact, hyperactivity might mean that you are not leading well at all. Leading by crisis will rarely get you to your treasure. Seasoned pirates are not afraid to risk looking like they know what they are doing by running a quiet, calm ship. They might not appear to be working as hard as some, but their crew will outperform any in the fleet.

Pirates and the Butterfly Effect

A pirate ship has much in common with a family system dynamic. Both are complex organizations comprised of constantly interacting and dynamic components, guided by norms and rules, and marked by self-regulation through feedback loops to maintain stability or encourage change. In both systems, the whole is greater than the sum of the parts, but a change in any individual part of the system, particularly one with power or control, can elicit a change in the overall system. Like any complex system, families and ships strive toward homeostasis, that is, stability in the midst of change.

Good pirates know that the only real power they have is over themselves. By extension, changing themselves inevitably changes the entire system. They know that small changes can lead to significant changes in seemingly remote or disconnected parts of the system. This phenomenon is called the *butterfly effect* by quantum scientists, who describe how the flapping of a butterfly's wing in Brazil can cause a storm in the Caribbean. Savvy pirates know that they can make conscious choices about who they are and how they function in the system that can, in turn, shift the entire system.

Pirates know several ways to use the butterfly effect. They can decide to poke the system and wait for the desired change. By adding a minor disruption, which can be as simple as asking a provocative question, they can change the everyday patterns. This minor shift can be enough to move people in a new direction with less resistance.

Another technique is using *Appreciative Inquiry* to poke a system for positive change. The power of this strategy lies in simply asking members of the organization positive questions. Every group has a general behavioral tendency, but also exhibits a continuum of behaviors. Asking group members, for example, what they do brilliantly instead of what they do poorly will turn the focus from what is wrong to what is right. The group will start to move in the direction of what they do well. The group can then successfully build on their own positive deviance.

Another way to prod the system is called *changing the dance*. Imagine that you have the same habitual way of interacting with your queen, another pirate, or member of your crew, particularly regarding some touchy subject. Every time that special subject comes up you each do your prescribed dance and end up in the same entrenched positions. You can see it coming, hear the music start, but it seems like you cannot stop yourself from joining the dance. With practice, a good pirate can stop the pattern and shift the dance.

To begin changing the dance, you first become aware of nuances. You notice the particular positions you tend to take immediately before the dance begins and the feelings that guide you into your battle station. Rather than stepping robotically into your traditional stance, you consciously ignore the emotional drivers and change your rhythm and moves. If you always step forward, begin with a backward step. If you typically speak loudly, try whispering. If your traditional step is detailed explanation, force yourself to keep quiet and ask for the other's opinion. And listen to the answer. Your shift will interrupt lockstep patterns and transform another's dance. Suddenly, you are both moving in new directions. When you use this approach, you stop playing to win. Instead, you play to match, and you shift the entire dynamic. If they expect you to fight, give up. If they expect you to run, stand still. Then step back and watch the reaction. When you notice an interaction pattern that takes you where you do not want to go, you change the dance again. Remember the old adage: If you always do the same thing, you always get the same results. Try poking the system by consciously doing the unexpected.

Use Yer Letters of Marques

Pirates establish their status as pirates and never forget who they are. Good ones have obtained official *Letters of Marques*, a license from the queen to sail on behalf of her kingdom. Pirates know that their freedom stems from their status and from their trust that every circumstance comes with options and opportunities.

When you begin practicing as a pirate, you can use your reputation to leverage your options. You build a reputation for making things happen by taking risks and being an adventurer. And you can earn more freedom, connections, and respect by playing on your reputation. It is O.K. to have fun and brandish your pirate card a bit. At the party without an invitation: "Of course I'm crashing this party, I'm the pirate." At the planning meeting: "Of course, I'm changing the rules, I'm a pirate." On the way to the retreat: "Of course, I'm not following the fleet, I'm a pirate." Even at the queen's ball: "Of course, I'm not wearing the naval uniform, I'm a pirate." You get the idea.

When and How to Mutiny

Pirates undertake two types of mutiny. The first is overt mutiny, in which the crew is rallied to take over the ship or storm the castle. This is a serious enterprise and is undertaken only in the most extreme circumstances. Once the decision to mutiny is made, there is no turning back. And everyone loses in a mutiny gone bad. Direct mutiny is called for only when the ship or your ethics are at risk. After a mutiny, your life and that of your crew is never the same. You have burned your bridges; you cannot return. Do this if you must, but be aware of the cost.

The indirect mutiny is more subtle and variable. Given a problematic directive, you might choose how, if, or when to obey. You can choose which orders to follow and which to postpone in any given moment. Your moral compass will help you choose. Any action that points toward murky moral waters or that aims your ship onto a shallow reef should give you pause. If the order is disagreeable but not immoral, you may not want to overtly refuse or rebel. But you may choose to manage the agenda by controlling the pace and method of how you fulfill all or part of the campaign. Sometimes you do just enough to fulfill the spirit of the order. Sometimes you take control of the timetable for action. Sometimes you act, but you redefine the method of response.

Savvy pirates are intensely aware of their motives and behaviors when undertaking any sort of mutiny. They make certain that their indirect mutinies are not acts of passive aggression or insubordination. They do not resist for the sake of resistance or to exert power. They act to take control of the *hows* in their life and to steer clear of dangerous waters.

No Raping or Pillaging

Pirates do not believe in zero-sum games. They know that more gold will always be found, new grog will flow, and more adventures will come. Good pirates do not have to suppress or steal from others to reach their own treasure. Oprah Winfrey did not become successful by bashing other daytime talk shows. She set her sights on what she wanted to achieve and went for it. She did not have to take anything away from someone else to get hers. She gives generously from her treasure chest, and her wealth keeps flowing.

Good pirates do not step over dead bodies to reach their treasure, and good captains do not build success by oppressing their crew. No organizational agenda, treasure trove, or queen's favor is worth risking the crew's health, sanity, or goodwill. With one eye on the good of the ship and the queen's agenda, the noble captain keeps another eye on the good of each crew member. Similarly, noble queens look after the best interests of the kingdom as well as the needs of their loyal subjects.

Good pirates do not confuse fear with respect. They know that killing the crew's spirit will never lead to treasure or loyalty. They know that a crew who follows their captain only out of fear will turn on him at the least sign of weakness. They know that if someone is too afraid to talk to them, they will miss indispensable information. They know that if people are motivated from fear, they cannot be good lighthouses. Savvy pirates operate in accordance with the old maxim: "The people you step over when you are moving up won't catch you when you are falling down."

Take Yer Due

Everyone deserves to make a good living, and pirates have no problem commanding a good livelihood. They know they deserve to be successful, and they act from that belief. They avoid the erroneous trap that holds some people and even entire organizations in irons, of thinking it is inappropriate to ask for what you need. A savvy pirate knows that you tend to get what you ask for or take, and little more. So pirates say, "Ask BIG!" If you deserve a raise, set your sights, make your case, and do not back down. If you need help, boldly ask for it. If your department is ignored, conjure the attention it needs. If you fail to ask for what you want, you must take responsibility for your unmet needs.

At the same time, wise pirates know that asking does not guarantee instant receipt. But they act from knowing that there are always multiple ways to get what you want. Sometimes the act of asking reveals what you need to improve or change to get what you seek. You might learn that you have not framed your request in accordance with the queen's strategic plan. You might learn that you need to work more closely with your crew so they can support your request. Or you might realize that your ship is not capable of receiving, because you have not gone into dry dock lately to scrape off your barnacles. Maybe you discover that you have not taken sufficient pains to train your crew or honor the queen or build relationships at court. Or maybe, you discover that you need to go to pirate finishing school and learn to be a better sailor or captain before you can gain the treasure you truly desire. Nevertheless, pirates are not dissuaded by impediments, large or small. Regardless of the obstacle they must circumnavigate to reach success, pirates stay the course tenaciously until they reach their treasure.

In our study of pirate wisdom, we have come to see that the lesson of getting clear about our treasure is the hardest pirate principle to practice consistently. Too often, we find that when we are not getting what we say we want, we have not been honest with ourselves. We catch ourselves professing our treasure to be what we believe we *should* want or what we wanted at a different phase of our lives. To avoid this brand of self deception, we find it helpful to remember to check our inner compass, and ask whether our aims and actions match our treasure.

When pirates are true to their treasure, they have no qualms about stating their desires. They also recognize that when they catch themselves sailing aimlessly around the same cove or rearranging the deck chairs on the poop deck for the third time in a month, they have lost sight of their treasure. It may be time to polish the résumé, put it in a bottle, and throw it out to sea. It might be time for a new ship, or it might be that a new challenge on the old ship is the solution. Either way, the pirate wastes no time in charting a course to the next grand adventure. Pirates know there are a million ways to live and prosper in this short spit of a life we have to sail.

Take Piratically Wild Risks

Successful pirates enjoy a reputation for taking wild risks and pulling them off successfully. There are two secrets to accomplishing the wild risk. First, wild risks are in fact scrupulously calculated. The act may look unpracticed, but in fact, it is based on cumulative expertise that substantially reduces apparent risk. Pirates are lifelong learners who build steadily on their experiences to gain ever-increasing knowledge and competence.

Second, for a wild risk to be successful, it must be implemented with boldness and surety. Robert Greene makes this point in *The 48 Laws of Power*. He states that boldness and hesitation elicit very different responses from the world around you: "Hesitation puts obstacles in your path, boldness eliminates them" (p. 228). Bold moves make you seem larger and more powerful, and weak moves solicit attack. Greene says that when you back down or hesitate, "you bring out the lion even in people who are not necessarily bloodthirsty."

Savvy pirates set themselves apart by intrepid acts. One way pirates cultivate a personal brand of risk taking is by attending to things they do that surprise or intrigue people. They capitalize on experiences that are in any way unconventional, even relatively simple acts like speaking a foreign language, taking snowboarding lessons, or escorting 25 high schoolers on an out-of-town field trip. These may seem to be tame talents if you have them, but they represent wild risks for others. The pirate sees that you can start with what makes you distinctive and amplify your distinction. If you can plan a dinner party for friends, you can orchestrate a major fundraising event. If you can order dinner in a second language, you can play host to international clients. If you can ride your bike around the neighborhood and write letters on Sunday afternoons, you can bike the hills of Italy on a wine tour and write a travelogue on your adventure. Above all, do not play small. Be audacious, and no one can resist you.

> *What you can do or think you can do, begin it.*
> *For boldness has magic, power, and genius in it.*
> —Johann Wolfgang von Goethe

Chapter 8

Pirates and Queens

An essential part of the queen's role is to provide protection for her fleet. She recognizes that in shifting seas, pirates will need to come back to port for supplies, shelter, rejuvenation, and to exchange unfit or unhappy crewmembers for new shipmates. The wise queen knows what each pirate needs and how to broker with them for service and treasure in exchange for safe passage and shelter.

The queen recognizes that pirates can be worthwhile sources of information, resources, and innovation for the kingdom. Pirates can bring a flow of news from faraway lands and serve as eyes on what goes on in other kingdoms. Pirates are useful for testing new waters and new ways of doing things. Because pirates are risk takers, they can serve as the queen's vanguard for exploring new territory. If the business queen has a concept for a new product or service, she might give it to her pirate group first for development and testing. The pirate on such an expedition enjoys freedom of movement under the queen's shield, and the queen carries the ultimate responsibility for the venture. The stakes are high for both pirate and queen, but the arrangement plays to each of their strengths.

A wise queen also recognizes that pirates can be valuable assets because they do not play the court sycophant role. Pirates deal in truths, even when the truth is unpopular or unwanted. Pirates may not freely volunteer their thoughts, but when pressed, they will be forthright. Thus a pirate can be useful as a sounding board for provisional plans and a candid barometer of happenings. If everyone else is saying, "Brilliant idea, your majesty," or, "Everything is going fine," and the pirate says, "You might want to consider an alternative," or "There is a stink down below," the wise queen knows to investigate or change course. And when a venture goes wrong, the pirate helps the queen save face by taking responsibility or blame.

While cognizant of pirates' value, the queen also knows they come at a price. Pirates can make great demands and can be disruptive or mavericks. Still, the queen knows that a harbored pirate is safer for her kingdom than one who is unpledged. The wise queen knows how to negotiate with even the most unruly pirates by granting them just enough freedom to seek their preferred treasure while supporting only those pirate ventures that contribute to her kingdom's best interests.

The queen also recognizes the danger of appearing too friendly with her pirates and risking the loss of their respect or of cultivating jealousy or distrust from within the court or from other queens. So she keeps the pirate at arm's length and may even reprimand or scold him in public. Over time, if the pirate proves true, the queen may allow him to come inside the castle on occasion. But the queen never forgets that a pirate cannot be tamed and that a pirate's heart is not for sale. In exchange for safe harbor, a good queen requires loyalty, allegiance, respect, and treasure from the pirates she harbors. She knows she is playing with fire, but she also knows that if she manages her pirates well, the entire kingdom benefits.

Chapter 9

Maintaining Safe Port

*The superior man, when resting in safety,
does not forget that danger may come.
When in a state of security he does not forget the possibility of ruin.
When all is orderly, he does not forget that disorder may come.*
—Confucius

All pirates need a safe port from which to come and go. A port offers resources, refuge, and rest in times of need. But each port has its benefits and its costs. Pirates know that no port is free and that no single port is universally reliable. So savvy pirates cultivate safe port on many shores.

Garnering Safe Port From the Queen

From the pirate's perspective, the queen's port is one of the safest, but also one of the most costly. To dock at the queen's harbor, a pirate must always be a gem in the queen's crown. Pirates do this by alternating between solving problems for her, supporting her plans, and bringing her treasure. Savvy pirates are judicious in asking the queen for boons. They know that their success on the queen's behalf builds their political credit, but asking for favors depletes that credit. So they are careful to avoid overdrawing their account with the queen.

One treasure pirates give to the queen is honesty, but they give it with reserve. Pirates never lie to their queen, and they are often among the few at court who can disagree with the queen and avoid her wrath. Still, pirates keep their own counsel about unpopular or sensitive information and share it only when it is ready for the queen's ears. Good pirates will not lie, but they may stay out of the queen's questioning sight when dealing with touchy issues, or they may forget to mention a detail that they know would trigger her response. Pirates choose when to be noticed by the queen. And they never mistake the queen for a friend. They know that friendly acts are not the same as friendship. Most important, they never ask the queen questions about issues in which they do not want her involvement. They know that asking a question opens the door for a command, which may force them into a precarious choice between doing something undesirable or denying the queen's wishes.

When confronted with an unpalatable directive, savvy pirates do not tell the queen that her proposal is mistaken or unwanted unless they are pressed for an opinion. They may not, however, rush forward to implement the charge. For example, the queen may become enthralled with the idea of owning a circus and ask the pirate to get her one. If the pirate sees no value in this venture, he does not argue, but neither does he go out and start buying elephants. First, the pirate does his homework. He finds out why the queen wants a circus. Do all the other queens have one? What is it that the circus represents or will offer the queen? Is there something better that would fulfill her desires? If he finds that there is no dissuading her from the notion, the pirate might suggest that they bring in other partners to share the risk because the resource demands will be high. He may point to someone whom he privately thinks needs marooning as the perfect person to lead this project. Or he may suggest bringing in a consultant to help develop a circus-acquisition plan. If the circus deal falls apart, the queen can chalk this up as "one that got away," without feeling like a failure or being forced to look for a scapegoat. The pirate always takes the blame and gives the queen a way to save face if a venture fails. A good pirate never brings bad news to the queen without a gem to go with it.

Garnering Safe Port From Others

Pirates know the power of allies, and they nurture a strong network of friends and associates. They live by the rule that one should have a friend in every port and an eye in every court. Pirates cultivate their network by attending to how their strengths and treasures correspond to the interests and needs of others. In every interaction, whether on their ship, at court, or on land, pirates note the interests, talents, treasures, and needs of the person with whom they are interacting. This may seem calculating, but it is more of a strategic cataloguing of features like tall, short, blond, dark, and it is one that is done instantly and constantly. In his bestseller documenting the phenomenon of rapid cognition, *Blink*, Malcolm Gladwell shares compelling research about our deeply rooted propensity to instantaneously assess patterns and details in our environment and make snap—and often amazingly accurate—judgments about everything from art forgeries to leadership ability to the probability of a marriage surviving. Gladwell's research suggests that some individuals make more accurate snap judgments than others, but that we all can become more cognizant and stronger masters of our instantaneous impressions and the decisions we make under stress.

Pirates have a strong nose for nuances of human nature: what makes someone tick, what underlies habits and behaviors and gets to the heart of the person. They pay attention to details, develop their skills of rapid cognition, and learn to judge situations and people quickly. They start with firm knowledge of themselves, so they can quickly assess how their treasures and talents align with those around them. And they build networks of people who complement their strengths and weaknesses. Pirates make sure that their contributions and unique characteristics are noticed, not by being ostentatious or self-aggrandizing, but by being engaging and conveying a personal style with aplomb.

Pirates know that their reputation is their foundation of safe port with others. Like a good savings account, pirates build their reputation by making contributions to others and keeping their commitments. They secure their investment with humility and gratitude for what they receive in return. They know that if they are truly good at what they do, they need not waste time convincing others. A good pirate's reputation sails ahead of the ship. At the same time, pirates know the double-edged sword of reputation. Pirates know that popularity, status, and success can make them vulnerable to attacks of jealousy from those with a need to prove their superiority or fawning from freeloaders who only want to ride their wake. Pirates value freedom more than reputation, so they are suspicious of people who are either overly competitive or excessively impressed with them. They do not fall victim to the siren songs of rivalry or flattery.

Garnering Safe Port With Fellow Pirates

Periodically, pirates need to find safe port with fellow pirates or recharge themselves at Dry Tortugas. Here they find their only true peer group, people with whom they can step out of the captain or pirate or queen role for a break away from the daily grind of the ship. Savvy pirates are highly selective about whom they include in their Dry Tortugas network. They know this most intimate group does not include all their peers or even all their friends. For this inner circle, they choose the most faithful pirate sisters and brothers with whom they trust their lives and to whom they would go without hesitation when called. On their ships, good pirates are tight-lipped about their fears, issues, and problems, but they need a tight circle of trustworthy friends with whom they can unfurl their sails and let their troubles flow out to sea.

Trusted pirate friends away from your ship are as a valued as any treasure. Because they understand you, they can help you find your solutions; because they care about you, they can offer you solace. They get you back on course when you go adrift; they help you navigate through dangerous waters. When it is time to move on, these are the folks who help you find a new ship.

Keep Yer Own Private Island

Sometimes a pirate's safest port is a private one. Time may not allow a vacation on Dry Tortugas, or friends may not be at hand. Sometimes pirates simply need to be alone and slow down enough to recheck their float plan, consult their maps, or simply listen to their soul talking. The trick is to know your personal symptoms of when you are losing your balance or missing vital personal nutrients or acting out of integrity with your true course. If you notice yourself thinking that your ship cannot sail without you, or if you cannot stop thinking about your work, you may be stalled by the magnetic pull of job identity attraction. Such disequilibrium sends your internal compass spinning and is a good indication that you need some solo reflection time on your own private island to get grounded.

Solitude is a healthy island on which pirates reflect on where they are in relation to their treasure goals and how well they are performing in their chosen roles. Just as when going into dry dock, pirates on their private island take a personal inventory of their readiness to sail: Have I attended to the basics: swimming every day, trimming my sails, caring for myself as well as my ship and crew? Have I mastered all the skills I need to provide my own safe port? Do I know how to build a life raft in an emergency or how to hitch a new ride if needed? Am I effective in my current position, or do I need to improve or change roles? Can I separate myself from my ship, shipmates, and daily work? Am I sailing in the right direction and with the right shipmates? Is this still the best ship for me, or is it time for a new ship?

Pirates find safe port in themselves by staying sharp in body and mind, and by remaining unattached to where they sailed yesterday. A pirate cannot rest on the illusionary security of the current sea they are in. They know to avoid investing so deeply in any one system or ship or crew or queen that they cannot move as political tides change. They know that their personal savings account is filled through adaptability, innovation, and creativity. Pirates' only security comes from building personal equity and keeping their investments diversified. To stay on course, pirates must take time to seek safe port with themselves and check their personal investments.

We don't see things as they are,
we see them as we are.
—Anais Nin

Chapter 10

X Marks The Spot

*I did not wish to take a cabin passage,
but rather to go before the mast and on the deck of the world,
for there I could best see the moonlight amid the mountains.
I do not wish to go below now.*
—Thoreau

Remember Why You Want to be a Pirate

Being a pirate is about bravely seeking fulfillment and freedom within the boundaries of our working lives. Many of us spend large portions of our lives in organizations that are intrinsically focused on something other than personal meaning and joy. Pirate wisdom can help us make a life as well as a living within these organizations. The poet, philosopher, and honorary pirate Henry David Thoreau warned against "lives of quiet desperation" lived by the masses who resign themselves to uninspired existence. Pirates' days may be demanding and their chosen seas may prove turbulent, but pirates are never desperate nor resigned to mediocrity. Pirates greet the winds of destiny face first and steer their lives according to their greatest inspirations. Pirates *live* their lives!

At its core, pirate wisdom is the practice of living truthfully, living well, sharing your gifts, and doing things that matter to you. To pirates, freedom is oxygen for honest existence. Because freedom means following and expressing the idiosyncratic rhythm that beats within each person's heart, a pirate's ship plan must be personally determined and privately executed. Thoreau's 150-year old call for following our personal compass still rings true: "If a man does not keep pace with his companions, perhaps it is because he hears a different drummer." Yet on days when you seem to awaken on some island of a life not of your making, your heart may echo the question that completes Thoreau's passage: "If the condition of things which we were made for is not yet, what were any reality which we can substitute? We will not be shipwrecked on a vain reality."

As you practice principles of pirate wisdom, your goal is to avoid the rocky shoals of vain reality and the siren call of conventional treasure. The true path to your dreams is found neither by breaking *nor* conforming to the conventions of your companions, but rather by tracing the arrow of your inner compass. When norms or rules oppose your path, artfully navigate around them. When standards and traditions support you, use them well. Become tuned in to that magnetic force that steadies you in the face of crosswinds and keeps you the vigilant guardian of your days. Once again, the good pirate Thoreau helps point the way:

Only that day dawns to which we are awake.

Getting Yer Treasure

Pirates never appraise their worth using conventional measures of success, unless social achievement is their true treasure. Pirates do not climb the corporate ladder to seek peace. Savvy pirates know that power lies in making powerful choices about how to see the world and show up in it. They know how to command personal control over what they focus on, react to, and perceive as important around them. They know that the more interior their command center, the more immune they become to organizational power and its natural shifts. They know that as queen, captain, or member of the crew, their power lies in perceiving so clearly and acting so authentically that their identity is unmistakable and their course undeniable.

At the end of the day, pirates know that everything around them is a system to navigate, a world by which to be amused, a treasure to seek, and a game to play. Pirates recognize the universe of political dealings and know they cannot reach their target, be it personal fortune or a cure for world hunger, without navigating relationships. At their core, all politics are relationships, and all relationships hinge on paying attention to oneself and others. Politics are neither intrinsically hard nor dirty. Because organizational waters are suffused with politics, developing political savvy makes sailing much more fun and effective.

But more than surviving politics or acquiring treasure, being a pirate is about living a glorious life. If you do not wish to stay below deck taking a cabin passage in your life, we invite you to become a pirate! Come out onto the deck of the world. Climb the mast to where you can clearly see the *Land of What Is*, but where you also can peer out on the moonlit night over the sea of your greatest possibility. Don your pirate hat, chart your course, take the wheel of your ship, and cast off as you call out to the heavens:

Now bring me that horizon!

Resources

The Arbinger Institute (2002). *Leadership and Self-Deception: Getting Out of the Box*. San Francisco: Berrett-Koehler.

Joel A. Barker (1993). *Paradigms: The Business of Discovering the Future*. New York: HarperBusiness.

David Cordingly (1997). *Under the Black Flag, The Romance and Reality of Life Among the Pirates*. New York: Random House.

Robert Greene (2000). *48 Rules of Power*. New York: Penguin.

Gareth Morgan (1997). *Images of Organization*. Thousand Oaks, CA: Sage Publications.

Joan Duncan Oliver, (2005). *Happiness: How to Find It and Keep It*, London: Duncan Baird Publishers.

Harriet Rubin (1998). *The Princessa: Machiavelli for Women*. New York: Dell.

Margaret Wheatley (2005). *Finding Our Way: Leadership for an Uncertain Time*. San Francisco: Barrett-Koehler.

International Talk Like a Pirate Day. *http://talklikeapirate.com/piratehome.html*

Gore Verbinski, director (2003). *Pirates of the Caribbean: The Curse of the Black Pearl*. Jerry Bruckheimer Films in association with Walt Disney Pictures.

978-0-595-40558-9
0-595-40558-4

Printed in the United States
115345LV00001B/561/A